The Critical Composer

The CRITICAL COMPOSER

The musical writings of
Berlioz, Wagner, Schumann,
Tchaikovsky, and others

Edited by Irving Kolodin

Essay Index Reprint Series

 BOOKS FOR LIBRARIES PRESS
FREEPORT, NEW YORK

First Published 1940
Reprinted 1969

STANDARD BOOK NUMBER:
8369-1358-2

LIBRARY OF CONGRESS CATALOG CARD NUMBER:
72-93351

PRINTED IN THE UNITED STATES OF AMERICA

Table of Contents

Table of Contents

Foreword

The conviction that accomplishment in one field automatically confers upon its possessor sagacity and wit in all others is a belief generally respected in the modern world, especially in America. Merchants give benedictions to cultural projects, admirals comment learnedly on politics, movie actors are heeded when they give opinions on foreign affairs. Whether this is a malady peculiarly American has not been clinically charted, but the germ unquestionably finds a friendly host here.

From the appearance of this volume it would appear that some such confusion is also involved in it, that the opinions of such men as Berlioz, Schumann, Wagner, Wolf, Debussy and the rest (who are assuredly better known as composers than as critics) have been exhumed purely for the dazzle of their names. The inference would seem to be that the preferences of one of them for the music of another should be esteemed as meaningful simply because the words were written by a Liszt, say, rather than by a Hanslick.

I can disclaim such an intention by remarking, merely, that a man who wrote as much music as Wagner did had an understanding of the procedures and the effort by which a score is created which is not accessible to one whose approach to the art was essentially external. I am not contending that it is therefore a better, or more valid attitude—merely that it is an *individual* one, and worthy of attention. Certainly such translation into verbal terms of a music's effect as one finds in Wagner's wisely-flavored comments on the C sharp minor quartet of Beethoven does not need the additional force of being said by the composer of "Die Meistersinger". His writing conveys, in excelsis, the sensitivity to an art and a capacity for conveying that sensitivity in words which should be the basis of all critical effort.

However, that fusion is to be encountered less often in verbal literature on music than in any other critical genre. For one thing, there is the specialized vocabulary of music to stand between the average man of sense and perception, and the application of those qualities to music. For another, the character of music is such that it lends itself less to recreation in words than painting or sculpture. Generally speaking, the man with an easy mastery of language lacks the intimate association with a vast literature to assert an authority in this field, while the one who settles comfortably into the company of any musical experience only infrequently contributes as much, or more, than pure feeling to the sum of his impression.

Foreword

The writing on music of so gifted and versatile a man as Bernard Shaw is esteemed today not, primarily, because of his superior background or uncommon penetration, but rather, because of the rarity with which a mind of his alertness and resilience is directed to such a pursuit. His activity in the London of the '90s was a brief and merely a casual phase of his career, of doubtful influence on the contemporary public. But in a field largely populated by mediocrities and hacks, his works undoubtedly exercised an influence of importance on certain young men of promise, breaking a path for the writing that has come from such men as Newman and Tovey, even Turner, Blom and Abraham (in England alone). The lack of so saline an influence in American criticism may explain some of its shortcomings. Indubitably, Huneker and Henderson had their effect, but it was of rather a different sort. One can only conclude that the ability to talk sense about music is perhaps an even rarer faculty than the ability to talk sense about other subjects.

The distinction between the writing of the men cited above and those whose works are reprinted herein is a precise if tenuous one. The material of this book may be described as writing which emerges not from literary perceptions brought to bear on a musical experience, but from musical reactions expressed through words. There is a sense of the sounding stuff itself in such writing which one searches for in vain in the writing of other temperaments. Thus one can find in Schumann's salute to the early Chopin, an anticipation of many qualities in that composer which were to assert themselves only later in his career. Also, Wolf's estimate of Bruckner (for whom he had a predilection founded on his opposition to Brahms) has not been importantly amplified or modified in the half century since the words were written. Despite his disposition toward Bruckner, Wolf, as a musician intimately sensitive to the shape and balance of musical expression, could not ignore the structural weaknesses of Bruckner's writing, the disproportion and clumsiness of his architecture.

It may be contended that this same Wolf's estimate of Brahms was a specious one relative to the position to which Brahms had been elevated by the anti-Wagnerites; or that Debussy's sharp attacks on Wagner were due at least in part to the antipathy of a reticent man for one of the German's vast outspokenness. There is, no doubt, a similar temperamental disability at the basis of Tchaikovsky's continuous and even petulant decrying of Brahms. But these are hardly attitudes more aggressive or misguided than one encounters in the writings of critics not hampered by occupational bias or professional disagreement; and there is, in each instance, at least a core of judicious perception to support the attitude.

It is, indeed, rather remarkable that so much that is sound and pertinent endures to command our attention in the writings of these composers. However, it is a fact that virtually the only writing about music done in the first half of the nineteenth century that is still read today is that of Berlioz and Schumann. (A single exception is that of the Englishman Henry Chorley, which retains an interest for students largely because of his documentation of the musical community in Germany during the period of its greatest ascendancy.) It is not too much to say that between them they created the model of what informative criticism should be.

For it must be remembered that musical criticism as it is known today had its inception almost coincidentally with the careers of Berlioz and Schumann. The reasons for this may seem mysterious, but they are fairly apparent. Most potent of all was the circumstance that the daily grist of criticism, the thing that gives its practitioners subsistence, continuity, and audience—are public performances. And save for the opera house, there were few sources of such performance prior to the nineteenth century. That the term "piano recital" (or "recitals of piano music", as he phrased it) originated with Liszt, is a landmark in locating the first activity of this kind. Chamber and concert music had emerged from the ducal palaces to public attention only a short time before, and self-perpetuating groups such as the Royal Philharmonic Society were still struggling for acceptance. Consider, merely, that Spohr attracted attention to himself as the first conductor, in the modern sense, by using a baton (in 1820) and it may be seen that the materials of conventional criticism were taking shape only slowly.

It is doubtful, for example, that the monumental accomplishments of Bach would have been so little known to the public for nearly a century after his death had there been a body of critical influence as we know it today. One can scarcely credit the recorded evidence that the first biographical study of so conspicuous a figure in musical history did not appear until half a century after his death, in 1802. How much Schumann and Berlioz contributed to the establishment of a critical tone and procedure may be understood from the antique, stodgy writing in this volume by Johann Forkel, the limited acquaintance with other musical literature, the wholly provincial attitude. Beside this, the freshness and vitality of Schumann's response to the music of Schubert, the modernity and breadth of Berlioz's comments on the Beethoven symphonies are as voices of our time, speaking to us in accents at once communicative and recognizable.

One of the remarkable aspects of their twin activity is the independent beginning of their critical careers within the span of a few years. Berlioz began his critical association with the *Journal des Débats* (after a desultory career of half a dozen years with other publications) in 1835, retaining that post until 1863. Together with a group of friends, Schumann founded the *Neue Zeitschrift für Musik* in 1833, continuing his active participation in its editorship for a decade. One can hardly avoid the conviction that they were drawn to the pursuit of these careers not more by wilful desire or by conscious intent than through the existence of a contemporary situation which demanded their talents.

There were battles to be fought, reputations to be

established, paths to be cleared. Beethoven had completed his life's work but hardly was generally accepted
by the public; Schubert was scarcely even a name,
Chopin was only beginning his public career, there was
Berlioz in France to be encouraged, Schumann in Germany. It is rather less astonishing that two men of the
capacities of Berlioz and Schumann directed their attention to such work than that, at so critical a period
of musical development, there were two men of their
exceptional sensitivities at hand to propagandize as
they did.

There is a point in considering the process by which
they embarked on their careers. Similar though their
impulses were, no two backgrounds could have been
more disparate. Berlioz was virtually penniless when
he did his first writing in 1829 for *Le Correspondent*.
There were hardly more sources of income for a composer in those days than now (especially one of Berlioz's
flamboyant, controversial tendencies) and the cost of
producing his own works was sufficient to keep him in
a state of perpetual insolvency, even before he acquired
a wife in 1833. It was after the latter event that one
may discover Berlioz accommodating himself simulta-
neously to the editors of *Le Corsaire, L'Europe lit-
téraire, La Revue européene* and other publications.
Even after he won a permanent appointment as music
commentator for the *Débats* in 1835, pure necessity
compelled him to find as many other outlets for his
writing as possible. The fluctuating fortunes of these
caused him to hold tenaciously to his post on the *Débats*

for nearly thirty years, though his income from it could not have been more than 1500 francs a year.

Though Berlioz repeatedly bewailed the drudgery of this occupation, its daily procession of "insipidities", the endless necessity for writing "nothings about nothings", one is advised to accept these protestations guardedly. Certainly no man could have mustered the volatility and lightness of the "Evenings in the Orchestra" who was not devoted to the written word, jealous of the power it gave him, proud of his formidable ability to manipulate it. Even in his bitterest protests against the "punishment" of writing, he could summon the freshness of mind to say (quoted in Ernest Newman's introduction to "Evenings in the Orchestra"): "This is indeed the lowest depth of degradation! Better to be Finance Minister in a republic!" Merely the pleasure that Berlioz must have taken in that scoffing analogy should have repaid him for at least a part of the day's torture. One can only underscore the sentiment of Newman that: "The musical critics of each country ought to dine together once a year and drink to the memory of this incomparably brilliant member of their craft".

Schumann had no such pressing necessity as a springboard for a career of writing. His decision, as far as one can determine, was purely a product of an intellectual impulse, the product of nothing more than the conviction that there was a job to be done and that he should take the lead in seeing that it was done. He was not, as one might say, Hectored by the purely financial need of a Berlioz. There are, in his early letters, intimations of the enthusiasm that was the guiding spirit of his publication—apostrophes to Bach (in which "everything is written for eternity"), to Beethoven, even to Schubert (of whom, in writing to Wieck from Heidelberg in 1829, he says: "I have propagated Schubert-worship to a great extent here, where his name is hardly known").

Thus the boy of nineteen was in truth the father to the man. It was only two years later that he was hailing Chopin with the most repeated of musical salutations: "Off with your hats gentlemen—a genius!" in the *Allgemeine Musikalische Zeitung*—and scarcely four years before the *Neue Zeitschrift für Musik* was born of a group that met almost nightly in Leipzig. As Schumann recounted its emergence when a selection of his writings was published in 1854: "The musical situation was not then very encouraging in Germany. On the stage Rossini reigned, at the pianoforte nothing was heard but Herz and Hüntent; and yet but a few years had passed since Beethoven, Weber and Schubert had lived among us. It is true that Mendelssohn's star was ascending, and wonderful things were related of Chopin, but the deeper influence of these only declared itself afterwards. Then one day the thought awakened in a wild young heart: 'Let us not look on idly, let us also lend our aid to progress, let us again bring the poetry of art to honour among men!' " One could hope for no clearer statement of a creed, or a more illuminating indication of the purposes that motivated Schumann, even to the

9

source of his over-estimation of such transitory figures as Niels Gade and Sterndale Bennett. They were of the time, and sympathetic—qualities which in themselves were almost sufficient, in Schumann's estimation, to redeem all other failings.

Wagner's career as a writer on music partook, curiously, of elements represented in the activities both of Berlioz and Schumann. There were the early drab bitter days in Paris, the days of arrangements for *cornet à pistons,* in which he wrote out of pure economic need, such essays as the one reprinted in this volume concerning the production of *Der Freischütz,* and various papers for Schlesinger's *Gazette Musicale.* The latter connection arose out of Wagner's necessity to pay Schlesinger fifty francs for the publication of his setting of *The Two Grenadiers,* a sum of money quite beyond Wagner's purse. As he recounts it (in *Mein Leben*): "For the moment the point was to compensate Schlesinger for the fifty francs agreed upon, and he proposed that I should do this by writing articles for his *Gazette Musicale.* As I was not expert enough in the French language for literary purposes, my article had to be translated and half the fee had to go to the translator. However, I consoled myself by thinking I should still receive sixty francs per sheet for the work. I was soon to learn, when I presented myself to the angry publisher for payment, what was meant by a sheet. It was measured by an abominable iron instrument, on which the lines of the columns were marked off with figures; this was applied to the article, and after careful subtraction of the spaces left for the title and signature, the lines were added up. After this process had been gone through, it appeared that what I had taken for a sheet was only half a sheet."

However, Wagner's temperament was hardly suited for that of workaday criticism. Most of the writings that fill the numerous volumes of his collected prose works are either windy philosophical discussions of aesthetics (always relative to his own reforms and the problem of establishing their validity), exhortations to the German people, or tracts on the baleful influence of *Judaism in Music*. But in common with Schumann, Wagner had a splendid sensitivity to certain phases of music in respect to which he was possessed of an exceptional eloquence—primarily and enduringly, Beethoven, of whom he wrote with love and discernment as early as the *Gazette Musicale* era (in which appeared the suggestive *Pilgrimage to Beethoven*) and as late as the essay herein quoted, written on the occasion of Beethoven's centenary in 1870. And certainly his essay on conducting is the basis of all philosophic and aesthetic thinking on that subject, as, by repute, his actual performances were the pragmatic point of departure for a whole school of leaders descending from von Bülow and Levi.

Wolf's career as a critic, though chronologically brief, was long enough to establish him in the true line of Berlioz as a writer of zest and individuality functioning through an assured musical orientation. He was twenty-four when he began to write for the *Salonblatt*

(Vienna) in 1884, and had already served an apprenticeship as second kapellmeister under Muck at Salzburg in 1881. The musical situation of Vienna at the time was one that made it almost imperative for a critic to choose sides—though one suspects that his adoration for Wagner would have had such an issue even were there no anti-party (the Brahmsians) for Wolf inevitably to oppose. In sum one is attracted less to the body of Wolf's criticism for its justice or even temper than for the brilliance and facility of his thoughts on the occasional subjects of which he wrote with special sympathy and understanding—Beethoven, Liszt, Wagner, Bruckner—and with his sharp response to those inexhaustible sources of aggravation for every critic: conductors and the public.

Similarly Debussy, whose critical personality was as strong a reflection of his musical bias as Berlioz's or Schumann's. The feeling for a tone coloring, a harmonic flavor, a melodic inflection is aptly paralleled in his verbal scoring—such a light-fingered phraseology as the one in which he describes Richard Strauss as "no relation to The Blue Danube," or sympathizes with Siegfried Wagner's desire to carry on his father's tradition as "not quite as easy as taking over a haberdashery shop"—are the marks of a wit and littérateur whose place in music would have been a secure one had he written no music of distinction, though assuredly an infinitely slighter one than he enjoys today. It must be considered, in estimating the point and significance of Debussy's writing, that he began his career not as an

Foreword

impressionable, wild-eyed youth (Berlioz, Schumann, Wagner and Wolf all commenced in their twenties) but as an opinionated, mature man of nearly forty (in 1901), who had already created *L'Après-midi, Pelleas,* the Nocturnes for orchestra, and the string quartet. These facts are to be considered in his belittlement of certain songs by Schubert, and his Unfinished Symphony, Schumann's *Dichterliebe,* and virtually all of Brahms; but they also increase one's admiration for his enthusiastic commendation of many works by Strauss, Moussorgsky, Rimsky, and Stravinsky. And for all his impatience with Wagnerian formulae, Wagnerian bombast, and above all, Wagnerian imitation by his contemporaries, he responded ungrudgingly to the pure musical sorcery of the man, to the point indeed of describing *Parsifal* as "one of the loveliest monuments of sound ever raised to the serene glory of music".

Of the other composers represented in this volume, none of them made of writing about music a steady occupation or a source of important income. Liszt's *Hommage à Chopin* is at once an act of faith and a superb recreation of a musical voice by the one man of all his acquaintances best qualified to do it. Gluck's statement of purpose is a unique documentation of an important development in musical procedure, anticipating by almost a hundred years the theory of music drama which Wagner achieved with more practicality if with no less conviction of aesthetic justice. Gounod's enthusiasm for Mozart, his sensitive definition of the necessities involved in the proper performance of that

13

composer's work will warm many hearts not so affected by Gounod's own music. And lastly, the quotations from Tchaikovsky's correspondence have been utilized (in preference to endless correspondence by many other composers) not only because his letters were in many cases lengthy literary compositions, but also because the association with Mme. von Meck impelled him to put into words detailed and considered impressions which, under other conditions, would have been expressed in evanescent conversation. Beyond all this, the amazing facets of his personality, his infinite capacity for examination of himself *contra* any figure of the past or present that occurred to him in a given moment are expressed in a language at once vigorous and characteristic.

This volume would be incomplete without an acknowledgment of the invaluable aid, in compiling and transcribing the material herein reprinted, of Mrs. Elizabeth Davies, and my wife, Irma Kolodin. Their collaboration was as intelligent as it was conscientious, and in both respects irreproachable.

IRVING KOLODIN

The Critical Composer

On Palestrina

By Charles Gounod

I went, usually, on Sunday to hear High Mass at the Sistine Chapel, frequently accompanied by my friend, Hérbert.* But the Sistine—to speak of it as it deserves, too much cannot be said of the authors of both what one sees and hears there—or rather, of what was once heard there in former days; for alas! although one may still see the sublime work of Michelangelo—destructible and already very much changed—it seems that the music of the divine Palestrina no longer resounds under those vaults that the political captivity of the sovereign pontiff has rendered mute, and which mourn eloquently in emptiness the absence of their holy guest.

I went, therefore, as often as possible to the Sistine Chapel. The music there—severe, ascetic, horizontal, and calm as the line of the ocean, anti-sensuous, and nevertheless, possessing an intensity of contemplation that sometimes amounts to ecstasy—produced at first a

* An excerpt from Gounod's *Mémoires*.

strange, almost unpleasant, effect upon me. Whether it
was the character of the composition itself, entirely new
to me, or the especial sonority of those particular voices,
heard for the first time, or, indeed, that attack, firm to
harshness, that forcible hammering that gives such
strong relief to the various entrances of the voices into
a web so full and close, I cannot say, but, at any rate,
this impression, however strange it might have been,
did not displease me. I went the second time, and still
again, and finished by not being able to do without it.

There are works that must be seen or heard in the
places for which they were created. The Sistine Chapel
is one of these exceptional places, unique of its kind in
the world. The colossal genius who decorated its
vaulted ceiling and the wall of the altar with his match-
less conceptions of the story of Genesis and of the Last
Judgment, the painter of prophets, with whom he
seemed to be on an equality, will doubtless never have
his equal, no more than Homer or Phidias. Men of this
stamp and stature are not seen twice upon the earth;
they are syntheses, they embrace a whole world, they
exhaust it, they complete it, and what they have said
no one can repeat after them.

The music of Palestrina seems to be a translation
in song of the vast poem of Michelangelo, and I am
inclined to think that these two masters explain and
illustrate each other in the same light, the spectator
developing the listener, and reciprocally, so that, finally,
one is tempted to ask if the Sistine Chapel—painting
and music—is not the product of one and the same

inspiration. Music and painting are there found in a union so perfect and sublime that it seems as if the whole were the twofold expression of one and the same thought, the double voice of one and the same hymn. It might be said that what one hears is the echo of what one sees.

There are, in fact, between the works of Michelangelo and Palestrina such analogies, such a similarity of ideas, that it is very difficult not to conclude that these two privileged beings were possessed of the same combination of qualities, and I was about to say, of virtues. In both the same simplicity, the same modesty in the employment of means, the same indifference to effect, the same disdain of seductive attractions. One feels that the material agent, the hand, counts for nothing, and that the soul alone, unalterably fixed upon a higher world, strives only to express in an humble and subordinate form the sublimity of its contemplations. There is nothing, even to the general, uniform tone in which this painting and this music are enveloped, which does not seem created with a sort of voluntary renouncement of all colors. The art of these two men is, so to speak, a sacrament where the visible sign is no more than a veil thrown over the divine and living reality. Thus, neither one nor the other of these two grand masters fascinates at first. In everything else it is the exterior that attracts; but here, not so; one must penetrate beyond the visible and the sensual.

The hearing of a work of Palestrina produces something analogous to the reading of one of the grand pages of Bossuet. Nothing is noticed as you go along, but at the end of the road you find yourself carried to prodigious heights; the language, docile and faithful servant of the thought, has not turned you from your course nor stopped you in its own interest; and you arrive at the summit without rude shock, without turning from the way, and without accident, conducted by a mysterious guide who has concealed from you both himself and his methods. It is this absence of visible means, of worldly artifices, of vain coquetry, that renders the highest works absolutely inimitable. To attain to the same degree of perfection requires the same spirit by which they were conceived, and the same raptures by which they were dictated.

On Beethoven

By Hector Berlioz

It is thirty-six or thirty-seven years ago, that, at the *Concerts Spirituels* * of the Opera, the trial was made of the works of Beethoven, then completely unknown in France. No one could imagine at the present day the reprobation at once heaped upon this admirable music by the majority of artists. It was strange, incoherent, diffuse; studded with crude modulations and wild harmonies, bereft of melody, of an exaggerated expression, and too noisy; besides being horribly difficult.

In order to meet the conditions set down by the men of taste who then controlled the Royal Academy of Music, M. Habeneck found himself obliged to make, in the very same symphonies the execution of which he organized and directed with so much care later on at the Conservatoire, monstrous cuts; such as, at the

* Since *A Travers Chant*, from which these comments on Beethoven symphonies have been taken, was published in 1862, this date would be 1825.—Ed.

very most, might be permissible in a ballet by Gallemberg, or an opera by Gaveaux. Without these *corrections* Beethoven would not have been admitted to the honor of figuring in the program of the *Concerts Spirituels* between a bassoon solo and a flute concerto.

At a first hearing of the passages marked with red pencil Kreutzer ran off, stopping his ears; and it required all his courage to make up his mind to listen to the *remaining portion* of the Symphony in D (No. 2), at other rehearsals. Let us not forget that the opinion of M. Kreutzer was, at that time, also that of ninety-nine out of every hundred musicians in Paris; and that, without sustained effort on the part of the insignificant fraction* who held a contrary view, the greatest composer of modern times would most likely be scarce known to us even yet. The mere fact, therefore, of the execution even of fragments of Beethoven at the Opera was one of great importance; to judge of which we have only to reflect that, without it, the Society of the Conservatoire would not have been constituted. It is to this small body of intelligent men, and to the public, that the honor of calling such an excellent institution into existence must be accorded.

The public—that is to say the "real" public, in the sense of *that which does not belong to any coterie* and which judges by sentiment and not according to the narrow ideas and ridiculous theories which it has

* A nineteenth century equivalent, in music, of the "passionate few" to whom Arnold Bennett attributed the establishment of most worthwhile literary works in his little book.

formed upon the subject of art—this public which, in spite of itself, makes mistakes, as is proved by the fact of its frequently having to alter its decisions was, at the very onset, struck by some of the eminent qualities of Beethoven. It does not ask whether such and such a modulation bears a due relation to some other one; whether certain harmonies are admitted by the *magisters;* or whether *it is permitted* to employ certain rhythms, previously unknown. It simply perceives that these rhythms, these harmonies and modulations, set off by a noble and passionate melody, and clothed in powerful instrumentation, make a strong impression upon it, and in an entirely new way. Could anything further be necessary to excite its applause?

Our French public experiences only at rare intervals the lively and ardent emotion of which musical art is capable; but, when it falls to its lot to become thoroughly agitated thereby, nothing can equal its gratitude to the artist, whoever he may be, to whom this is due. From the moment of its first appearance, the celebrated allegretto in A minor of the Seventh Symphony, which had been inserted in the Second in order to help to *pass off the remainder,* was appreciated at its value by the public of the *Concerts Spirituels.* The pit rose in a body with vociferous cries for its repetition; and, at a second performance, the first movement and the scherzo of the Symphony in D, which had not been much enjoyed on the occasion of the first trial, met with an almost equal success.

The manifest interest which from that time the public began to evince with regard to Beethoven doubled the strength of his defenders; and reduced, if not to silence at least to inaction, the majority of his detractors.

Thus, little by little, thanks to those twilight rays which revealed to the far-seeing the direction in which the sun was about to rise, the seed developed and resulted in the foundation, almost expressly for Beethoven, of the magnificent Society of the Conservatoire, at the present day with scarcely a rival in the world.

SYMPHONY NO. 3, IN E FLAT
(The "Eroica")

It is extremely wrong to tamper with the description placed at the head of this work by the composer himself. The inscription runs: "Heroic Symphony to celebrate the memory of a great man." In this we see that there is no question of battles or triumphal marches such as many people, deceived by mutilations of the title naturally expect; but much in the way of grave and profound thought, of melancholy souvenirs and of ceremonies imposing by their grandeur and sadness —in a word, it is the hero's *funeral rites*. I know few examples in music of a style in which grief has been so consistently able to retain such pure form and such nobleness of expression.

The first movement is in triple time and at a degree of speed nearly equal to that of the waltz. But, nevertheless, what can be more serious or more dramatic than this allegro? The energetic theme which forms its foundation does not at first present itself in its entirety. Contrary to custom the composer, in commencing, has only allowed us a glimpse of his melodic idea; it does not present itself in its full effect until after an exordium of some bars. The rhythm is particularly remarkable by the frequency of syncopation and by combinations of duple measure; thrown, by accentuation of the weak beat, into the triple bar. When, with this disjointed rhythm, rude dissonances come to present themselves in combination, like those we find near the middle of the second repeat, where the first violins strike F natural against E (the fifth in the chord of A minor) it is impossible to repress a sensation of fear at such a picture of ungovernable fury. It is the voice of despair, almost of rage.

Still, it may be asked—why this despair? Why this rage? The motive of it does not appear. The orchestra becomes calm at the following bar; as if, exhausted by the excess to which it had given way, its strength began suddenly to fail. Moreover, the phrases are now gentle; and we find in them all that remembrance is capable of suggesting to the soul of the nature of sad regrets.

It is impossible to describe or even to indicate, the multitude of melodic and harmonic aspects in which Beethoven reproduces his theme; we will confine ourselves to the mention of one which is extremely strange, which has formed the text of many discussions, and which the French editor corrected in the score, imagining it to be a mistake of the engraver; but which was, later on, reinstated—as the result of more ample information.

The first and second violins alone hold, in tremolo, the major second B flat, A flat (part of the chord of the dominant seventh in E flat); when a horn, having quite the appearance of being at fault and of coming in four bars too soon, starts timidly with the commencement of the principal theme; running exclusively on the notes—E flat, G, E flat, B flat. One may imagine the strange effect produced by this melody, formed of the three notes of the tonic chord, against the two dissonant notes of the chord of the dominant; notwithstanding the harshness being much reduced by separation of the parts. But, at the moment when the ear is inclined to revolt against such an anomaly, a vigorous tutti interrupts the horn; and, concluding *piano* on the tonic chord, allows the violoncellos to return; who then state the entire theme with its natural harmony. Looking at things broadly it is difficult to find a serious justification for this musical caprice.* They say, however, that the composer was very strenuous upon the point; and it is even related that, at the first rehearsal of this symphony, M. Ries being present stopped the orchestra by calling out—"Too soon! too soon!— The horn is wrong!" and that the only reward for his zeal

* To this Berlioz appends the note: "Whichever way we look at it, if the above is really an intention of Beethoven, and if there is any truth in the anecdotes which are current upon the subject, it must be a whim amounting to absurdity."

On Beethoven

was that he received from Beethoven, who was furious, a sharp lecture.

No other eccentricity of this nature is to be found in the rest of the score; and the Funeral March is a drama in itself. We seem to trace in it the translation of those beautiful lines of Virgil on the funeral procession of the young Pallas—

Multa que praeterea Laurentis praemia pugnae
Adgerat, et longo praedam jubet ordine duci.
Post bellator equus, positis insignibus, Aethon
It lacrymans, guttis que humectat grandibus ora.*

The end, especially, is profoundly moving. The march-theme reappears; but in fragments, interspersed by silence, and without any other accompaniment than three notes *pizzicato* by the double bass. When these shreds of the lugubrious melody thus alone, bare, broken and effaced, have one by one passed on to the tonic, and the wind instruments raise a cry which is the last adieu of the warriors to their companion in arms the entire orchestra dies away on the organ-point, *pianissimo*.

The third movement is entitled Scherzo, according to custom. In Italian the word signifies "play," or "humorous frolic." At first sight it does not appear obvious how such a style of music can figure in an epic composition. To realize this it must be heard. The rhythm

* And so they gathered the many spoils of the battle of Laurentum and ordered that the booty be paraded in a long procession. When the glorious prizes had been arranged, Aethon the warrior horseman marched and wept, and the earth was soaked with heavy tears.

27

and the movement of the scherzo are, indeed, there. There is also play; but it is play of funereal kind, at every instant clouded by thoughts of mourning—a kind of play, in fact, recalling that which the warriors of the Iliad celebrated round the tombs of their chiefs.

Even in the most capricious evolutions of his orchestra Beethoven knew how to preserve the grave and somber tint, as well as the profound sadness which ought naturally to dominate in such a case. The *finale* is nothing but a development of the same poetic idea. One very curious passage of instrumentation is to be remarked at the commencement; showing what effect can be drawn from the opposition of different *timbres.* It is a B flat taken by the violins, and repeated immediately by the flutes and oboes; in the style of an echo. Although the repercussion takes place on the same note of the scale, at the same movement and with equal force, so great a difference results from this dialogue that the nuance which distinguishes the instruments from one another might be compared to that between *blue* and *violet.* Such refinements of tone-color were altogether unknown before Beethoven; and it is to him that we owe them.

The finale, though so varied, consists entirely of a very simple *fugato* theme; upon which the composer afterwards builds, in addition to numerous ingenious details, two other themes; one of the latter being of extreme beauty. The outline of this melody does not enable one to perceive that it has, so to speak, been extracted from another one. Its expression, on the contrary, is much more touching; and it is incomparably more graceful than the first theme, the character of which is rather that of a bass—a function which it fulfills extremely well. This melody reappears shortly before the close, in a slower degree of movement, and with new harmonies, by which the effect of its sadness is increased. The hero causes many tears; but after the last regrets paid to his memory, the poet turns aside from elegy; in order to intone with transport his hymn of glory. It may be somewhat laconic but this peroration rises to a high effect and worthily crowns the musical monument. Beethoven has written works more striking perhaps than this symphony; and several of his other compositions impress the public in a more lively way. But it must be allowed, notwithstanding, that the "Sinfonia Eroica" possesses such strength of thought and execution, that its style is so emotional and consistently elevated besides its form being so poetical, that it is entitled to rank as equal to the highest conceptions of its composer.

A sentiment of sadness not only grave but, so to speak, antique takes possession of me whenever I hear this symphony although the public seem indifferently touched by it. We must deplore the misfortune of an artist who, consumed by such enthusiasm, fails to make himself sufficiently well understood, even by a refined audience, to insure the raising of his hearers up to the level of his own inspiration. It is all the more sad as the same audience, on other occasions becomes ardent, excited or sorrowful along with him. It becomes seized

with a real and lively passion for some of his compositions; equally admirable, it may be admitted, but nevertheless not more beautiful than the present work. It ap-
preciates at their just value the allegretto in A minor of
the Seventh Symphony; the allegretto scherzando of
the eighth; the finale of the fifth and the scherzo of the
ninth. It even appears to experience emotion at the
funeral march of the symphony of which we are now
speaking (the "Eroica"); but, in respect of the first
movement, it is impossible to indulge in any illusion;
for twenty years of observation tend to assure me that
the public listen to it with a feeling approaching cold-
ness, and appear to recognize in it a learned and energetic composition, but nothing beyond that.

No philosophy is applicable to this case; for it is
useless to say that it has always been so, and that everywhere the same fate has befallen all high productions
of the human mind. Also that the causes of poetic emotion are secret and inappreciable, that the conception
of certain beauties with which particular individuals are
gifted is absolutely lacking in the multitude, or that it
is even impossible that it should be otherwise. All that
is of no consolation. It does not calm the indignation
with which one's heart is filled—an indignation instinctive, involuntary, and it may even be, absurd—at
the aspect of a marvel which is misunderstood; of a
composition so noble which is regarded by the crowd
without being perceived; listened to without being understood; and allowed to pass by without courting any

attention, precisely as if it were a mere case of something mediocre or indifferent.

Oh! it is frightful to be obliged to acknowledge with a pitiless conviction, that what I find beautiful may constitute *beauty* for me, but that it may not do so for my best friend; that he, whose sympathy generally corresponds with my own, may be affected in a totally different way; and that even the work which affords me a transport of pleasure—which excites me to the utmost, and which moves me to tears, may leave him cold; and may even cause him displeasure and annoyance.

The majority of great poets have little feeling for music, and enjoy only trivial and childish melodies. Many highly intellectual people who think they love it have little idea of the emotion it is able to raise. These are sad truths; but they are so palpable and evident that nothing but the illusion caused by certain systems can stand in the way of their recognition. I have observed a dog bark with pleasure on hearing a major third, executed *sostenuto* by double-stopping upon the violin; but the offspring of the same animal were not in the least affected, either by the third, fifth, sixth or octave —or, in fact, by any chord whatever, whether consonant or dissonant. The public, however it may be composed, is always, in respect to great musical conceptions, in a similar position. It has certain nerves which vibrate in sympathy with certain forms of resonance. But this organization, incomplete as it is, is unequally distributed; as well as subject to no end of modifications. It follows that it would be almost foolish to count upon such and such artistic means in preference to others for the purpose of acting upon it. Thus the composer is best advised to follow blindly his own individual sentiment; resigning himself beforehand to the results which chance may have in store.

One day I was coming out of the conservatoire with three or four amateurs; the occasion being a performance of the "Choral" Symphony.

"What do you think of that work?" said one of them to me.

"Immense! Magnificent! Overpowering!"

"That is singular. For my part, I found it cruelly tiresome. And you?" added the speaker, addressing an Italian.

"Oh! as for me, I find it obscure; or rather unpleasant, for there is no melody."

But, besides that, note the different views which several journals express about it:

"The Choral Symphony of Beethoven represents the culminating point of modern music. Art has hitherto produced nothing to be compared with it in respect of nobleness of style, grandeur of plan and refinement of detail."

(Another journal)—"The Choral Symphony of Beethoven is a monstrosity."

(Another)—"This work is not altogether lacking in ideas; but they are badly disposed and the general effect is incoherent and devoid of charm."

(Another)—"The Choral Symphony of Beethoven

contains some admirable passages; though it is evident that the composer lacked ideas and that, his exhausted imagination no longer sustaining him, he made considerable effort, and often with some success, in order to replace inspiration by artistic resources. The few phrases which we meet with in it are handled in a superior manner and disposed in a perfectly clear and logical order. On the whole, it is the highly interesting work of a *used-up* genius."

Where shall we find the truth or where the error? Everywhere, and yet in no particular place. Each one is right; for what is beautiful for one is not so for the other. This naturally follows, if only from the fact that one has experienced emotion whilst the other has remained unaffected; that the first has received a lively enjoyment, whilst the second has suffered an intense fatigue. What can be done in such a case? Nothing. But it is distressing, and makes me feel inclined to prefer the foolish view of beauty being absolute.

SYMPHONY NO. 5, IN C MINOR

The most celebrated of all is also, without question, in our opinion, the one in which Beethoven gives free scope to his vast imagination; without electing to be either guided or supported by any outside thought; in the first, second and fourth symphonies he more or less extended forms which were already known; investing them with the poetry of a brilliant and passionate inspiration due to his vigorous youth. In the third (the

"Eroica") the form tends to a greater breadth, it is true; the thought also reaching to a greater height. Notwithstanding all this, however, we cannot fail to recognize therein the influence of one or other of those divine poets to whom, for so long, the great artist had erected a temple in his heart. Beethoven, faithful to the precept of Horace:

Nocturnâ versate manu, versate diurnâ,*

used to read Horace habitually; and, in his magnificent musical epic which, rightly or wrongly, is said to have been inspired by a modern hero, remembrances of the antique Iliad play an admirable and beautiful, but no less evident part.

The Symphony in C minor, on the other hand, appears to us to emanate directly and solely from the genius of Beethoven. It is his own intimate thought which is there developed; and his secret sorrows, his pent-up rage, his dreams so full of melancholy oppression, his nocturnal visions and his bursts of enthusiasm furnish its entire subject; whilst the melodic, harmonic, rhythmic and orchestral forms are there delineated with an essential novelty and individuality, endowing them also with considerable power and nobleness.

The first movement is devoted to the expression of the disordered sentiments which pervade a great soul when prey to despair. It is not that calm and concentrated despair which bears the outward appearance of

* Study carefully by night and day.

resignation; or the grief, so somber and silent, which
Romeo evinces on hearing of the death of Juliet. Rather
is it the terrible fury of Othello, when receiving from
the mouth of Iago the empoisoned calumnies which
persuade him of Desdemona's crime. Sometimes it is a
frenzied delirium, bursting forth in fearful cries. Sometimes it is an excessive depression, expressing itself
only in accents of regret and seeming to hold itself in
pity. Listen to those orchestral gasps; to those chords
in dialogue between wind and strings, which come and
go whilst gradually growing weaker, like the painful
respiration of a dying man. These at last give place to
a phrase full of violence; in which the orchestra seems
to rise again reanimated by a spark of fury. See that
quivering mass; which hesitates for an instant, and then
precipitates itself, bodily divided, into two ardent uni-
sons, resembling two streams of lava. And, then having done this, say whether this passionate style is not
both beyond and above anything which had yet been
produced in instrumental music.

This movement presents a striking example of the
effect produced by the excessive doubling of parts
under certain circumstances, and of the wild aspect
of the chord of the fourth on the second note of the
scale; otherwise described as the second inversion of
the chord of the dominant. It is met with frequently
without preparation or resolution, and it even occurs
once without the leading note and on an organ point;
the D forming the bass of the strings, whilst the G

forms the discordant summit of a few parts assigned to the wind.

The adagio presents some characteristic relation with the allegretto in A minor of the Seventh Symphony; and with that in E flat of the fourth. It offers equally the melancholy gravity of the first and the touching grace of the second. The theme, first stated by the violoncellos and violas, together with a simple *pizzicato* double-bass accompaniment, is followed by a certain phrase for wind instruments which recurs continually in the same form and in the same key from one end to the other of the movement, whatever may be the successive modifications to which the original theme is subject. This persistence of one and the same phrase, in adhering always to its original simplicity, is so profoundly sad that it produces, little by little, upon the soul of the listener an impression impossible to describe, but which is certainly the most powerful of its kind which we have ever experienced.

Among the boldest harmonic effects of this sublime elegy may be quoted:

(1) The *sostenuto* of an upper part on the dominant B flat whilst the strings move rapidly below; passing by the chord of the sixth (D flat, F, B flat), to which the said upper part does not belong.

(2) The incidental phrase executed by flute, oboe and two clarinets, proceeding in contrary motion and giving rise from time to time, to unprepared discords of the second between G, the leading note, and F, as major sixth in the key of A flat. This third inversion of

the chord of the seventh on the leading note is forbidden by most theorists, precisely as the upper pedal just mentioned; though it does not, on that account, present any less delightful effect. There is also, at the last entry of the original theme, a *canon in the unison at one bar distance* between violins and flutes, clarinets and bassoons. This would give to the melody thus treated a new interest, were it possible to hear the imitation of the wind instruments; but, unfortunately, just then the entire orchestra is playing so loud as to render it inaudible.

The scherzo is a strange composition, the first bars of which, though presenting nothing terrible, cause that strange emotion we are accustomed to experience under the magnetic glance of certain individuals. Everything in it is mysterious and somber; the orchestral devices, with more or less sinister aspect, seeming to belong to the same order of ideas which created the famous Bloksberg scene in Goethe's "Faust." Tints of *piano* and *mezzo-forte* prevail throughout. The middle part, or trio, is remarkable for a bass passage executed with all the force of the bow; the uncouth weight of which shakes the very feet of the players' desks and resembles somewhat the gambols of a delighted elephant.* But the monster departs, and the noise of his mad careering gradually dies away. The motive of the

* Saint-Saëns had, perhaps, this remark in mind when he utilized the "Dance of the Sylphs" (from Berlioz's "Damnation of Faust") on the double-basses in his "Carnival of the Animals" to suggest elephants.—Ed.

scherzo now reappears in *pizzicato;* peace is gradually restored; until nothing more is heard than a few notes, daintily plucked by the violins, and the faint clucking produced by the bassoons, giving their high A flat, closely opposed by G, as octave in the chord of the dominant minor ninth. Then, interrupting the cadence, the stringed instruments *col arco* softly take the chord of A flat, upon which they repose for a length of time. The rhythm is entirely dependent upon the kettledrums, by which it is sustained in the form of light strokes given by sponge-covered sticks; its design thus appearing in dull form against the general stagnation of the rest of the orchestra.

The kettledrum note is C, and the key of the movement that of C minor; but the chord of A flat, long sustained by the other instruments, seems, on the one hand, to introduce a different tonality, whilst, on the other, the isolated *martellato* of the kettledrum on C tends to preserve the sentiment of the original key. The ear hesitates, uncertain as to the way in which this harmonic mystery is about to issue; when the dull pulsations of the kettledrum, becoming more and more intense, meet the violins who have now rejoined the rhythmic movement and changed the harmony. The chord is now that of the dominant seventh (G, B, D, F,) throughout which the kettledrums obstinately continue their roll upon C tonic. And then it is that the entire orchestra, reinforced by the trombones which have hitherto not appeared, bursts forth in the major mode upon a triumphal march-theme, and the *finale* begins.

Everybody knows the effect of this thunder stroke; and it is, therefore, useless to detain the reader with any account of it.

The critics have nevertheless tried to detract from the merit of the composer by declaring that, in the above, he had resorted to a mere vulgar procedure; the brightness of the major mode pompously succeeding the obscurity of the minor *pianissimo*. Also, that the triumphal theme was lacking in originality, and that the interest grew less as the end was approached, instead of following a contrary order.

To this we may reply by asking:

> Was less genius necessary to create such a work because the passage from *piano* to *forte* and that from *minor* to *major* were means already known?

How many other composers have resorted to the same means, and how far can the results which they have obtained be compared to this gigantic song of victory; in which the soul of the poet-musician, henceforth free from all hindrance and earthly suffering, seems to rise beaming towards the very heavens? The first four bars of the theme are, it is true, not of great originality; but the forms of the fanfare are naturally restricted; and we do not believe it would be possible to discover new ones without altogether emerging from the simple, grand and pompous character which is proper to it. Beethoven, therefore, required only a fanfare entrance for his *finale;* and, throughout the rest of the movement, and even in the part succeeding the principal phrase, he retains the elevation and novelty of style which never abandons him. As to the reproach of not having proceeded with an increasing interest to the conclusion the following may be replied:

> Music cannot, at all events in the state in which we know it, produce a more violent effect than that of the transition from the scherzo to the triumphal march. It was, therefore, quite impossible to proceed with any augmentation of it.

To *sustain* such a height of effect is, in fact, already a prodigious effort. Notwithstanding the amplitude of the developments in which Beethoven has indulged, he has succeeded in accomplishing this. But this very equality between the commencement and conclusion suffices to cause a *suspicion* of decrease, on account of the terrible shock which the nerves of the listener experience at the opening. Nervous emotion, thus raised to its most violent paroxysm, becomes immediately afterwards so much the more difficult to effect. In a long row of columns of similar height an optical illusion causes those which are most removed to appear smaller than the rest. Possibly our feeble organization would be better suited to a laconic peroration such as:

Notre général vous rapelle,

by Gluck. The audience would, in this way, not have time to grow cold; and the symphony would finish before fatigue had intervened to prevent the possibility of accompanying the author in his advance. This observation, however, only applies, so to speak, to the *mise-en-scène* of the work; and by nò means prevents this finale from being in itself of a magnificence and richness in comparison with which there are few pieces which could appear without being completely crushed.

SYMPHONY NO. 7, IN A

The Seventh Symphony is celebrated for its allegretto. This does not arise because the other three parts are any less worthy of admiration; far from it. But the public does not generally judge by any other measure than that of effect produced; and, as it only measures this effect by the amount of applause, it follows that whatever is most applauded always passes for being the most beautiful, notwithstanding that there are beauties of infinite worth which are not of a nature to excite any demonstrations of approval. Then it happens, that, in order to promote still further the object of this predilection, all the rest is sacrificed to it. Such is, at all events, in France the universal custom. That is why in speaking of Beethoven, one says: the "Storm" of the "Pastoral" Symphony; the "finale" of the Symphony in C minor; the "andante" of the Symphony in A, and so on.

It does not appear to be certain that the latter was composed after the "Pastoral" or "Eroica" symphonies. Several authorities hold, on the contrary, that it preceded these symphonies by a certain period of time. The mere number which designates it as the *seventh* would, consequently, should this opinion be well founded, refer merely to the order of publication.*

The first movement opens with a broad and pompous introduction, in which melody, modulations and orchestral designs successively compete for the hearer's interest; besides commencing with one of those effects of instrumentation of which Beethoven is incontestably the creator. The entire mass, striking a chord both loud and short, discovers an oboe during the silence which succeeds. The entrance of this oboe, hidden by the orchestral attack had not been previously perceived; and it now states the opening melody in *sostenuto*. No more original mode of opening could be imagined. At the end of the introduction the note E (as dominant of A), recalled after several excursions into neighboring keys, becomes the object of a play, of tone-color between violins and flutes somewhat analogous to that met with in the first few bars of the finale of the "Eroica" Symphony. The E comes and goes without accompaniment during six bars; changing its aspect each time it passes from string to wind. Finally, retained by the flute and oboe, it serves to join the introduction to the allegro; and becomes the first note of the principal theme, of which it gradually outlines the rhythmical form. I have heard this subject ridiculed on account of its rustic simplicity. Probably the reproach of lack of nobleness would never have been applied to it had the author, as in the "Pastoral" Symphony,

* There is no basis for this conjecture in the knowledge of Beethoven that we now possess.—Ed.

placed at the head of his allegro in plain letters the inscription:

"RONDE DE PAYSANS"; *(Peasants' Rondo)*.

We therefore see that, if there are listeners who prefer *not* to be warned of the subject treated by the musician, there are others, on the contrary, indisposed to welcome any idea presented to them in an unaccustomed dress, unless they are told beforehand of the reason of the anomaly. In default of being able to decide between two such dissimilar opinions it seems that the artist, in such a case, can do no better than follow his own sentiment; without foolishly straining after the chimera of popular suffrage.

The phrase in question is of a rhythm extremely marked; which, afterwards passing to the harmony, is reproduced in a multitude of aspects without arresting its cadenced march until the end. The employment of a rhythmic form in *ostinato* has never been attempted with so much success; and this allegro, the extensive development of which runs constantly upon the same idea, is treated with such inconceivable sagacity, the changes of tonality are so frequent and ingenious, the chords are formed into groups and enchainments of such novelty, that the movement concludes before the attention and ardent emotion which it excites in the listener have had time to lose anything of their extreme vivacity.

The harmonic effect most seriously blamed by the partisans of scholastic discipline, and at the same time the most successful one, is that of the resolution of the discord in the chord of six, five, on the subdominant in the key of E natural. This discord of the second, placed in an upper part against a loud tremolo between the first and second violins, is resolved in a way altogether new. One resolution might have allowed the E to remain, and have caused the F sharp to rise to G; whilst another might have kept the F, whilst causing the E to fall to D. Beethoven uses neither one nor the other of these. Without changing his bass he brings the two parts of the discord together, in an octave on F natural, by making the F sharp descend a semitone and the E a major seventh. The chord, therefore, which was previously one of six, five, now becomes a minor sixth; its fifth having disappeared from F natural. The sudden change from *forte* to *piano* at the precise moment of this singular harmonic transformation both gives it a more decided aspect and renders its grace twofold.

Let us not forget, before passing to the next movement, to mention the curious crescendo by means of which Beethoven reintroduces his favorite rhythm, which he had for an instant abandoned. It is produced by a two-bar phrase:

D, C sharp, B sharp, B sharp, C sharp

in the key of A major; repeated, eleven times in succession at a low pitch, by the basses and violas; whilst the wind instruments hold E, above, below, and in the middle, in quadruple octave; and whilst the violins keep on delivering, as a sort of chime, the notes:

E, A, E, C sharp,

the percussions of which continually increase in speed and are combined in such a way as to present the dominant when the basses are at D or B sharp; and the tonic whenever they play C sharp. This is absolutely new; and no imitator has, I think, yet tried very happily to apply this beautiful discovery.

The rhythm, which is one as simple as that of the first movement, although of different form, is equally the principal cause of the incredible effect produced by the allegretto. It consists exclusively of a dactyl followed by a spondee; which occur without ceasing, sometimes in three parts, sometimes in a single one, and sometimes in the whole of the parts together. Sometimes they serve as an accompaniment, often attracting a concentrated attention to themselves, or furnishing the first theme of a small episodic double fugue for the stringed instruments. It appears at first for the lower strings of the violas, violoncellos and double basses, marked with a simple *piano;* with the intention of being soon afterwards repeated in a *pianissimo* full of melancholy and mystery. From there it passes to the second violins; whilst the violoncellos chant a sort of lamentation in the minor mode; the rhythmical phrase continuing to rise from octave to octave, and thus arriving at the pitch of the first violins. These, by a crescendo, transmit it to the wind instruments in the upper region of the orchestra; where it then bursts forth in all its force. Thereupon, the melodious plaint being stated with greater energy, assumes the character of a convulsive lamentation; irreconcilable rhythms painfully agitate one against another; for these are tears, and sobs and supplications—in short, the expression of a grief without limit and of a devouring form of suffering. But a gleam of hope has just appeared; these agonizing accents being succeeded by a vaporous melody, pure, simple, soft, sad and resigned; like *patience smiling at grief.* Only the basses continue their inexorable rhythm under this rainbow of melody; and it seems, if I may borrow a quotation from English poetry, like:

> *One fatal remembrance, one sorrow, that throws*
> *Its black shade alike o'er our joys and our woes*

After a few alternations remindful of anguish and resignation the orchestra, as if fatigued by such a painful struggle, presents only fragments of the original theme, and dies away exhausted. The flutes and oboes take up the theme, with a murmuring voice, but strength fails them to finish it; and it is the violins to which the termination falls, in a few notes of *pizzicato,* scarcely perceptible. Afterwards, with a flicker of fresh animation, remindful of the flame of a lamp which is about to die out, the wind instruments exhale a profound sigh upon an indecisive harmony, and *all is silence.* This plaintive exclamation, with which the andante both commences and concludes, is produced by

a chord (that of the 6-4) which has a continual tendency to resolve upon some other; and the incomplete
harmonic sense of which is the only one which could
permit its use for the purpose of finishing in such a
way as to leave the hearer with a vague impression and
to augment the feeling of dreamy sadness in which the
whole of the preceding must necessarily have plunged
him.

The subject of the scherzo is modeled in quite a
new style. It is in F major; and instead of concluding
its first section in C, or B flat, or D minor, or A minor,
or A flat, or D flat, after the habit of the great majority
of pieces of this kind, it is upon the key of its *third*—or
in other words upon A natural major—that the modulation falls. The scherzo of the "Pastoral" Symphony,
which is also in F, modulates into D major, a third
lower. There is some resemblance in the color presented by this contrast of keys; but this is not the
only affinity to be observed as existing between the two
works. The trio of the present movement (*presto meno
assai*), in which the violins hold the dominant almost
continually, whilst the oboes and clarinets execute a
genial rustic melody below, is altogether within the
sentiment of the landscape and the idyll. We meet in
it also a new form of crescendo, stated in a lower part
of the second horn, which murmurs the two notes

A, G sharp

in duple rhythm, although the bar is of three beats;
and accentuates the G sharp, although A is the integral

note. The public seems always struck with astonishment on hearing this passage.

The finale is at least as rich as the preceding movements in new combinations, piquant modulations and capricious charm. The theme presents a certain relation with that of the overture of "Armide"; but it is only in the arrangement of the first few notes, and is more evident to the eye than to the ear; for, when executed, nothing can be more dissimilar than these two ideas. We should better appreciate the freshness and coquetry of Beethoven's phrase, so different from the cavalier-spirit of Gluck's theme, if the chords taken in upper parts by the wind instruments were less dominating over the first violins singing in the medium register, whilst the second violins and violas accompany the melody below with *a tremolo* in double-stopping. Throughout the course of this *finale* Beethoven has drawn effects as graceful as they are unforeseen from the sudden transition from the key of C sharp minor to that of D major. One of his happiest bold harmonic strokes is unquestionably the great pedal on the dominant E; set off by a D sharp of a value equal to that of the principal note. The chord of the seventh is also sometimes introduced above in such a way that the D natural of the upper parts falls precisely upon the D sharp of the basses. One might expect the result of this to be a horrible discord; or at all events, a deficiency of clearness in the harmony. Nothing of the kind happens, however; for the tonal force of this dominant is such that the D sharp does not affect it in any way, and the bourdon (bass) of E continues exclusively to be heard. Beethoven did not write his music for the mere purpose of being looked at.

The coda which is introduced by this threatening pedal is of extraordinary brightness, and well worthy of terminating such a masterpiece—alike of technical ability, taste, fantasy, knowledge and inspiration.

SYMPHONY NO. 9, IN D (THE "CHORAL")

To analyze such a composition is a difficult and dangerous task, and one which we have long hesitated to undertake. It is a hazardous attempt, excuse for which can only lie in persevering efforts to place ourselves at the composer's point of view and thus perceive the inner sense of his work, feel its effect, and study the impressions which it has so far produced; both upon privileged organizations and upon the public at large. Amongst the many judgments which have been passed upon this work there are perhaps not even two which are identical. It is regarded by some critics as a *monstrous folly*. Others can only see in it the parting gleams of an expiring genius. A few, more prudent, confess that they do not yet understand it; but are hopeful of being able to appreciate it, at least approximately, later on. The great bulk of artists deem it to be an extraordinary conception; though some of its parts are not yet explained, and appear to have no direct object.

But there are a few musicians who are impelled by their nature to bestow every care in examining whatever may tend to increase the field of art. These have ripely reflected upon the general plan of the "Choral" Symphony; and after having read it and attentively listened to it on many occasions they are firm in the conviction that this work forms the most magnificent expression of Beethoven's genius. That opinion, as we have already hinted in these pages, is the one to which we adhere.

Without prying into what the composer may have wished to express in the way of ideas personal to himself in this vast musical poem, this being a search in favor of which the field of conjecture is equally open to everyone, let us see if the novelty of form is not here justified by an intention altogether independent of philosophic or religious thought, an intention as reasonable and beautiful for the fervent Christian as for the Pantheist or Atheist—an intention, in fact, purely musical and poetical.

Beethoven had already written eight symphonies before this. What means were open to him, in the event of his purposing to go beyond the point at which he had already arrived, by the unaided resources of instrumentation? *The junction of vocal with instrumental forces.* But in order to observe the law of crescendo, and to place the power of the auxiliary which he wished to give the orchestra in effective relief in the work itself, was it not necessary still to allow the instruments to occupy the foreground of the picture which he proposed to unfold? This proposition being once admitted, we can easily imagine him induced to adopt a style of mixed music capable of serving as connecting link between the two great divisions of the symphony. It was the instrumental "recitative" which thus became the bridge which he ventured to throw out between chorus and orchestra; and over which the instruments passed to attain a junction with the voices.

The passage being decided on, the author was obliged to make his intention clear by announcing the fusion which he was about to effect. Then it was that, speaking by the mouth of a Coryphée, he himself cried out, in employing the very notes of the instrumental recitative which he had just employed:

"O Freunde, nicht diese Töne! sondern lasst uns augenehmere anstimmen, und freudenvollere."*

In the above lies, so to speak, the "treaty of alliance" entered into between chorus and orchestra; the same phrase of recitative pronounced by one and the other seeming to be the form of an oath mutually taken. From that point, the musician was free in the choice of the text of his choral composition. It is to Schiller that Beethoven applies. He takes the poet's "Ode to Joy," colors it with a thousand tints which the unaided poetry could never have conveyed, and, right up to the end, he pursues one continual road of increasing pomp and grandeur and éclat.

Such is, probably, the reason, more or less plausible, of the general arrangement of this immense composition; the several parts of which we are now to study.

* "O Friends, not tones like these! But let us turn to others, more pleasant and full of joy."

The first movement, with its imprint of somber majesty, does not resemble any which Beethoven had previously written. The harmony is sometimes of an excessive boldness; and designs of the most original kind as well as features of the most expressive order meet, cross and interlace in all ways without producing either obscurity or encumbrance. On the contrary, the general result is *one* effect which is perfectly clear. The multitude of orchestral voices may complain or threaten, each one in its own peculiar way or special style. But they all seem to unite in forming one single voice; so great is the force of the sentiment by which they are animated.

This *allegro maestoso,* written in D minor, commences, however, upon the chord of A without its third; or, in other words, with a continuation of the notes A, E, placed as a fifth, and arpeggioed above and below by the first violins, violas and double basses, so that the listener does not know whether what he hears is the chord of A minor, that of A major, or that of the dominant of D. This prolonged indecision as regards tonality gives much force and dignity of character to the entry of the *tutti* on the chord of D minor. The peroration contains accents which move the soul completely; and it would be difficult to find anything more profoundly tragic than this song of the wind instruments under which a chromatic phrase in *tremolo* for the stringed instruments gradually swells and rises—grumbling the while, like the sea at approach of a storm. This is indeed a magnificent inspiration.

We shall have more than one occasion in the course of

this work to draw attention to aggregations of notes to which it is really impossible to give the name of chords, and it is as well to admit that the reason of these anomalies escapes us completely. Thus, at page 17 of the admirable movement of which we have just spoken, there is a melodic design for clarinets and bassoons, in the key of C minor, which is accompanied in the following way:

1. The bass takes F sharp (with diminished seventh harmony).

2. Then, A flat (with chord of three, four and augmented sixth).

3. Lastly, G (above which the flutes and oboes strike the notes, E flat, G, C, yielding a chord of six, four).

No. 3 would thus correctly resolve No. 2 if the second violins and violas did not persist in adding to the harmony the two notes, F and A flat; which so pervert it as to produce a very disagreeable confusion, though happily very short.

This passage is but lightly instrumented and is of a character altogether free from roughness; for which reason I cannot understand this quadruple discord, so strangely introduced without cause. One might suspect an engraver's error; but on examining these two bars and those which precede them, all doubt disappears; and the conviction arises that such was really the intention of the composer.

The *scherzo vivace* which follows contains nothing similar. We find in it, it is true, several pedals, both high and medium on the tonic; and which pass through the chord of the dominant. But I have already made my profession of faith on the subject of these holding-notes foreign to the harmony, and there is no need of this new example to prove the excellent help which can be drawn therefrom when they are naturally induced by the musical sense. It is by means of the rhythm especially that Beethoven has been able to imbue this charming *badinage* with so much interest. The theme, so full of vivacity when it presents itself with its fugal reply at a distance of four bars, literally sparkles with life, later on; when, the answer coming in a bar sooner than expected, by that means forms a three-bar rhythmic design, in lieu of the duple rhythm of the commencement.

The middle of the scherzo is taken up by a *presto à deux temps* (alla breve) of quite a country-like joviality, and of which the theme unfolds itself upon the intermediary pedals, either of tonic or dominant, and with accompaniment of a counter-melody which also harmonizes equally well with one or other of these two holding-notes. The song is introduced for the last time by an oboe phrase of delightful freshness; which, after having toyed for some time with the chord of the major ninth (dominant of D) disports itself in the key of F in a manner as graceful as it is unexpected. In this may be perceived a reflection of those gentle impressions so dear to Beethoven—impressions produced by the aspect of Nature smiling and calm, the purity of the air, or the first rays of dawn on a spring morning.

In the adagio cantabile the principle of unity is so

little observed that it might rather be regarded as two distinct pieces than as one. The first melody, in B flat and in common time, is succeeded by another melody, absolutely different from it, in triple time, and in D. Then the first theme, slightly altered and varied by the first violins, makes a second appearance in the original key, for the purpose of reintroducing the triple melody. This now appears without either alteration or variation in the key of G; after which the first theme definitively installs itself, and does not again permit its rival to share with it the attention of the listener.

Several hearings are necessary before one can altogether become accustomed to so singular a disposition of this marvelous adagio. As to the beauty of all these melodies, the infinite grace of the ornaments applied to them, the sentiments of melancholy tenderness, of passionate sadness and of religious meditation which they express, if my prose could give of all this even an approximate idea, music would have found in the "written word" such a competitor as even the greatest of all poets was never able to oppose to it. It is an immense work; and, when once its powerful charm has been experienced, the only answer for the critic who reproaches the composer for having violated the law of unity is:

So much the worse for the law!

We are now approaching the moment when the vocal and orchestral elements are to be united. The violoncellos and double basses intone the recitative, of which we have already spoken, after a ritornello of the wind

instruments as violent and rough as a cry of anger. The
chord of the major sixth (F, A, D) with which this
presto starts off is intruded upon by an appoggiatura
on the B flat, struck at the same time by flutes, oboes
and clarinets. This sixth note of the key of D minor
grates horribly against the dominant and produces an
excessively harsh effect. This is well expressive of fury
and rage; but I still do not quite see what it was that
excited the composer to this sentiment, unless, before
saying to his Coryphée:

> 'Let us turn to other tones more pleasant and full
> of joy',

he wanted, in virtue of some odd whim, to calumniate
instrumental harmony.

He seems to regret it, however, for, between each
phrase of the bass recitative, he quotes, as souvenirs
held in affection, fragments of the three preceding
movements; * and, moreover, after this same recitative,
he places in the orchestra, amid an exquisite choice of
chords, the beautiful theme which all the voices are
shortly about to sing to the ode of Schiller. This chant,
of calm and gentle character, becomes gradually more
animated and brilliant in passing from the basses, who
first announce it, to the violins and wind instruments.
After a sudden interruption, the entire orchestra resumes

* The conception of a "rejection section," in which Beethoven
tries in turn the basic idea of each previous movement before
settling on the chorale theme, had apparently not been established in Berlioz's time.—Ed.

the furious ritornello already mentioned, which now announces the vocal recitative.

The first chord is again placed on F; which is supposed to carry third and sixth. It does really carry them; but, this time, the composer is not contented with the appoggiatura B flat, for he adds E, G, and C sharp, so that ALL THE NOTES OF THE MINOR DIATONIC SCALE are played together, and produce the frightful assemblage:

F, A, C sharp, E, G, B flat, D.

The French composer Martin, says Martini, wanted, in his opera of "Sappho," about forty years ago, to produce an analogous effect, by employing, all at once, every diatonic, chromatic and enharmonic interval. This happens at the moment when Phaon's lover is about to throw herself into the waves; and without troubling about the suitability of such an attempt, and without asking whether or no this venture was an infringement on the dignity of art, we may be sure, at all events, that his object was not misunderstood. My efforts to discover that of Beethoven would, however, be completely useless. I perceive a formal intention—a calculated and thought-out project—to produce two discords at the two instants which precede the successive appearances of vocal and instrumental recitative. But, though I have sought high and low for the reason of this idea, I am forced to avow that it is unknown to me.

The Coryphée, after having sung his recitative, the words of which, as we have said, are by Beethoven himself, alone delivers the theme of the "Ode to Joy," to the light accompaniment of two wind instruments and strings *pizzicato*.

This theme appears right up to the end of the symphony; and is always recognizable, although its aspect changes continually. The study of these various transformations presents an interest so much the more powerful as each one of them gives a new and decided tint to the expression of one and the same sentiment—that of joy. This joy is, at first, full of gentleness and peace; but becomes somewhat more lively at the moment when the female voices make themselves heard. The time changes; the phrase first sung in common time now appears in 6-8 and, with continual syncopation; when it assumes a stronger character; becomes more agile; and, generally, approaches a war-like style.

This is the song of the hero sure of victory; we can almost see his armor sparkle and hear the sound of his measured step. A fugato theme, in which the original melodic design may still be traced, serves for a while as material for orchestral disportment—this representing the various movements of a crowd, active and full of ardor.

But the chorus soon returns, forcibly chanting the joyous hymn in its first simplicity; aided by the wind, which repeats the chords in following the melody; and traversed, in many ways, by a diatonic design, executed by the entire mass of strings, in unison and octave.

The *andante maestoso* which follows is a kind of chorale; first intoned by the tenors and basses of the chorus with one trombone, violoncellos and basses. The joy is now religious, grave and immense. The choir ceases for a moment, in order to resume its wide harmony with a lesser strength, after an orchestral solo producing an organ effect of great beauty. The imitation of the majestic instrument of Christian churches is produced by the flute lower register, the clarinet chalumeau, the lower sounds of the bassoon, the violas divided into high and medium parts, and the violoncellos playing upon their open strings G, D or upon C open string with its octave.

This movement begins in G; passing into C and then into F, and finishing by an organ-point on the dominant seventh of D. Following it is a grand allegro in 6-4 in which, from the very beginning, the first theme, already so variously produced, and the chorale of the preceding andante appear united. The contrast of these two ideas is rendered even more salient by a rapid variation of the joyous song, which is executed below the long notes of the chorale, not only by the first violins, but also by the double basses.

Now, it is impossible for double basses to execute a succession of notes so rapid; and no one has yet been able to explain how a man so skillful as Beethoven in the art of instrumentation could possibly forget himself so far as to write for this heavy instrument a feature of this kind.

There is less manliness, less grandeur and more lightness of style in the next movement; the substance of which presents a simple gaiety, first expressed by four voices alone, and afterwards warmly coloured by addition of the chorus.

Some tender and religious accents alternate, twice successively, with this gay melody; but the movement increases in precipitation. The whole orchestra breaks out; and percussion instruments, including kettledrums, cymbals, triangle and bass drum rudely mark the strong beats of the bar. Joy resumes dominion—popular and tumultuous joy, which would even resemble an orgy did not the whole of the voices, in terminating, pause anew upon a solemn rhythm, in order to send their last salute of love and respect to religious joy by an ecstatic exclamation. The orchestra finishes alone; but not without projecting from its ardent course fragments of the first theme, of which one cannot tire. . . .

This symphony is the most difficult of all by this composer; its performance necessitating study, both patient and repeated; but, above all, well directed. It requires, moreover, a number of singers greater than would otherwise be necessary; as the chorus is evidently supposed to cover the orchestra in many places; and, also, because the manner in which the music is set to the words and the excessive height of some of the vocal parts render voice production difficult, and diminish the volume and energy of the sounds produced.

Whatever may be said, it is certain that Beethoven, when finishing his work, and when contemplating the majestic dimensions of the monument he had just erected, might very well have said to himself:

Let Death come now, my task is accomplished.

By Robert Schumann

It should be written in gold letters, that on last Thursday the Leipzig orchestra performed—*all the four overtures to "Fidelio" one after another.* Thanks to ye, Viennese of 1805, that the first did not please ye, and that Beethoven, in divine rage therefore poured forth the three others. If he ever appeared powerful to me, he did so on that evening, when, better than ever, we were able to listen to him, forming, rejecting, altering, in his own workshop, and ever glowing with inspiration.

He was most gigantic in his second onset.* The first overture was not effective; hold! thought he, the second shall upset all your calculations,—and so he set himself to work anew, and allowed the thrilling drama to pass by, and again sang the joys and sorrows of his heroine. This second overture is diabolical in its boldness, still

---

* Schumann obviously wrote without the knowledge, now widely disseminated, that the overture known as the Leonore No. 2 was actually written first, and the "first" Leonore after it.—Ed.

bolder, in certain details, than the third, the well known great C-major. But it did not satisfy him; he laid this also aside, merely retaining certain passages, from which, already artistically quieter, he formed the third. This was afterwards followed by the more easy and popular one in E-major, which is generally heard at the theatre as an opening piece.

Such is the great Four-Overture work. Formed after the manner of Nature's formations, we first find in it the root basis, from which, in the second, the giant trunk arises, stretching its arms to the right and to the left, and finally completed by its airy crown of blossoms.

FLORESTAN

A-MAJOR SYMPHONY OF BEETHOVEN

Florestan began to talk, at the same time commencing the A-major Symphony. Said he: "I must laugh when I think of the dry old registrar, who discovered in this a battle of the giants, with a very effective annihilation of them all in the last movement, while he slyly passed over the allegretto, because it did not fall in with his fancy; and I must laugh at those who eternally preach about the innocence and absolute beauty of music; to be sure, art has no business to imitate the unlucky octaves and fifths of life—it should rather conceal them; yet in some consecrated arias (of Marchner's, for example) I often find beauty without truth, and in Beethoven (though seldom) sometimes truth without beauty. But

On Beethoven

I shiver to the finger-tips when I hear some people declaring that Beethoven gave himself up, while writing his symphonies, to the greatest sentiments—lofty thoughts of God, immortality and the course of the spheres; the genial man certainly pointed to heaven, with his flowery crown, but his roots spread broadly over his beloved earth.

"But—to return to the symphony. The idea is not mine, but taken from an old number of the musical paper, the 'Cecilia'; and was perhaps suggested by delicacy of feeling towards Beethoven, who was to be spared from entering some courtly hall or other.

"It is the merriest wedding, the bride, a heavenly maid with one rose in her hair. If I do not err, in the introduction the guests arrive, greeting each other with many bows; and the airy flutes remind us, that in the village gay with May bloom and ribbon favours, every one rejoices for and with the bride, Rosa. And if I am not mistaken her pale mother asks her, with a tremulous glance, 'Knowest thou not that we must part?' and then Rosa, overcome, throws herself in her mother's arms, yet draws the hand of her bridegroom with her. And now all is still in the village" (here Florestan broke into the allegretto) "only the butterflies float past, or a cherry blossom falls. The organ sounds; the sun rises high; the bells ring loudly; church-goers enter, one after the other; pew doors are opened and shut; countrymen study their hymn books; others look up to the choir; the procession comes nearer—first the choir boys, with lighted tapers and the incense, then friends, often turning round to look at the bridal pair accompanied by the priest, the parents, the bridesmaids, and all the young people of the village at last. They range themselves in order, the priest ascends the altar, and talks, now to the bride, then to the happiest of men; he tells them of the duties and aims of the sacred bond, he paints to them the joy that is found in virtuous love and peace—and as he demands 'yes' that embraces in it an eternity, and they respond, firmly, slowly—I cannot continue the picture—fancy the finale as you will!" Florestan broke off, and finished the allegretto so that it rang as though the sexton threw the door to, and it echoed throughout the church.

By Richard Wagner

If we consider the lives of Haydn and Mozart and
contrast them, we shall find a transition from Haydn
through Mozart to Beethoven with regard to the exter-
nals of life.* *Haydn* was and remained a prince's attendant, providing, as a musician, for the entertainment
of his master, who was fond of display; temporary in-
terruptions, such as his visits to London, changed but
little in the practice of his art, for in London also he
remained a musician recommended to and paid by men
of rank. Submissive and devout, he retained the peace
of a kind-hearted, cheerful disposition to a good old
age; the eye only that looks at us from his portrait is

* Wagner's long essay on Beethoven, of which this is an
excerpt, was written in 1870, to commemorate the hundredth
anniversary of the composer's birth. Wagner visualized himself as "called upon to deliver an oration at some ideal cele-
bration in honor of the great musician." He admitted,
however, that he expanded his thoughts much more than
would have been possible under such circumstances.—Ed.

65

filled with gentle melancholy. Mozart's life, on the contrary, was an incessant struggle for an undisturbed and secure existence such as he found it so peculiarly difficult to attain. Caressed when a child by half Europe, the youth found every gratification of his lively desires impeded in a manner akin to positive oppression, and from his entrance into man's estate he sickened miserably towards an early death. He finds musical servitude with a princely master unbearable, he gives concerts and "academies" with an eye to the general public, and his fugitive earnings are sacrificed to the petty enjoyments of life.

If Haydn's *Prince* continuously demanded new entertainment, Mozart was none the less compelled to provide novelties day by day to attract the *public;* fugitive conception, and ready execution acquired by immense practice, will, in the main, account for the character of both their works. Haydn wrote his noblest masterpieces in old age, when he enjoyed the comforts of a foreign as well as a home reputation. But Mozart never attained that: his finest works were sketched between the exuberance of the moment and the anxiety of the coming hour. Thus a remunerative attendance on some prince, as a medium for a life more favorable to artistic production, continually hovered before his soul. What his emperor withholds, a king of Prussia offers: Mozart remains "true to his emperor", and perishes in misery.

If Beethoven had made his choice of life after cool deliberation, keeping his two great predecessors in view, he could not have gone surer than he did in fact go under the *naïve* guidance of his natural character. It is astonishing to observe how everything here was decided by the powerful instinct of nature. This instinct speaks plainly in Beethoven's shrinking from a manner of life akin to Haydn's. A glance at young Beethoven was probably sufficient to deter any prince from the whim of making him his *Kapellmeister*. But the peculiar complexion of his character appears more remarkable in those of its features which preserved him from a fate such as Mozart's.

Like Mozart, placed without means in an utilitarian world, that rewards the Beautiful only inasmuch as it flatters the senses, and wherein the Sublime remains altogether without response, Beethoven could not at first gain the world's suffrage by the Beautiful. A glance at his face and constitution would make it sufficiently clear that beauty and effeminancy were almost synonymous to his mind. The world of phenomena had scanty access to him. His piercing eye, almost uncanny, perceived in the outer world nothing but vexatious disturbances of his inner life, and to ward them off was almost his sole *rapport* with that world. So the expression of his face became spasmodic: the spasm of defiance holds this nose, this mouth at a tension that can never relax to smiles, but only expand to enormous laughter. It used to be held as a physiological axiom that for high intellectual endowments a large brain should be enclosed in a thin delicate skull, to facilitate an immediate cognition of external things; nevertheless, upon the inspection of his remains some years ago, we saw, in conformity with the entire skeleton, a skull of altogether unusual thickness and firmness. Thus nature guarded a brain of excessive delicacy, so that it might look inwards and carry on in undisturbed repose the world contemplation of a great heart. This supremely robust constitution enclosed and preserved an inner world of such transparent delicacy, that, if left defenceless to the rough handling of the outer world, it would have dissolved gently and evaporated,—like Mozart's tender genius of light and love.

Now let any one try to realize how such a being must have regarded the world from within so massive a frame!

Assuredly the inner impulses of that man's Will could never, or but indistinctly, modify the manner in which he apprehended the outer world; they were too violent, and also too gentle, to cling to the phenomena upon which his glance fell only in timorous haste, and finally with the mistrust felt by one constantly dissatisfied. Nothing involved him in that transient delusion which could entice Mozart forth from his inner world to search after external enjoyment. A childish delight in the amusements of a great and gay town could hardly touch Beethoven; the impulses of his Will were too strong to find the slightest satisfaction in such light motley pursuits. If his inclination to solitude was nourished hereby, that inclination coincided with the independence he was destined for. A wonderfully sure instinct guided him in this particular respect and became the mainspring of the manifestations of his character. No cognition of reason could have directed him better than the irresistible bent of his instinct. That which led Spinoza to support himself by polishing lenses, which filled Schopenhauer with that constant anxiety to keep his little inheritance intact and determined his entire outer life, and which indeed accounts for apparently inexplicable traits of his character—*i.e.,* the discernment that the veracity of all philosophical investigations is seriously endangered when there is any need of earning money by scientific labor—*that* fostered Beethoven's defiance of the world, his liking for solitude, and the almost coarse predilections shown in his manner of life.

In point of fact Beethoven *did* support himself by the proceeds of his musical labors. But as nothing tempted him to strive for a pleasant life, there was less need for rapid, superficial work, or for concessions to a taste that could only be gratified by "the pleasing." The more he thus lost connection with the outer world, the clearer was his inward vision. The surer he felt of his inner wealth, the more confidently did he make his demands outwards; and he actually required from his friends and patrons that they should no longer *pay* him for his works, but so provide for him that he might work for himself regardless of the world. And it actually came to pass, for the first time in the life of a musician, that a few well-disposed men of rank pledged themselves to keep Beethoven independent in the sense desired. Arrived at a similar turning-point in his life,

Mozart perished, prematurely exhausted. But the great kindness conferred upon Beethoven, although he did not enjoy it long without interruption or diminution, nevertheless laid the foundation to the peculiar harmony, which was hence-forth apparent in the master's life, no matter how strangely constituted. He felt himself victorious, and knew that he belonged to the world only as a free man. The world had to take him as he was. He treated his aristocratic benefactors despotically, and nothing could be got from him save what he felt disposed to give, and at his own time.

But he never felt inclined for anything save that which solely and continually occupied him: the magician's disport with the shapes of his inner world. For the outer world now became extinct to him; not that blindness robbed him of its view, but because *deafness* finally kept it at a distance from his hearing. The ear was the only organ through which the outer world could still reach and disturb him; it had long since faded to his eye. What did the enraptured dreamer *see,* when, fixedly staring, with open eyes, he wandered through the crowded streets of Vienna, solely animated by the waking of his inner world of tones?

The beginning and increase of trouble in his ear pained him dreadfully, and induced profound melancholy, but after complete deafness had set in, no particular complaints were heard from him; none whatever about his incapacity to listen to musical performances; the intercourse of daily life only, which never had attracted him much, was rendered more difficult, and he now avoided it the more.

A musician without hearing! could a blind painter be imagined?

But we know of a blind *Seer*. Tiresias, to whom the phenomenal world was closed, but who, with inward vision, saw the basis of all phenomena,—and the deaf musician who listens to his inner harmonies undisturbed by the noise of life, who speaks from the depths to a world that has nothing more to say to him—now resembles the seer.

Thus genius, delivered from the impress of external things, exists wholly in and for itself. What wonders would have been disclosed to one who could have seen Beethoven with the vision of Tiresias! A world, walking among men,—the world *per se* as a walking man!

And now the musician's eye was lighted up from within. He cast his glance upon phenomena that answered in wondrous reflex, illuminated by his inner light. The essential nature of things now again speaks to him, and he sees things displayed in the calm light of beauty. Again he understands the forest, the brook, the meadow, the blue sky, the gay throng of men, the pair of lovers, the song of birds, the flight of clouds, the roar of storms, the beatitude of blissfully moving repose. All he perceives and constructs is permeated with that wondrous serenity which music has gained through him. Even the tender plaint inherent in all sounds is subdued to a smile: the world regains the innocence of its childhood. "To-day art thou with me in

Paradise." Who does not hear the Redeemer's word when listening to the Pastoral Symphony?

The power of shaping the incomprehensible, the never seen, the never experienced, in such wise that it becomes immediately intelligible, now grows apace. The delight in exercising this power becomes humor; all the pain of existence is shattered against the immense delight of playing with it; Brahma, the creator of worlds laughs as he perceives the illusion about himself; innocence regained plays lightly with the sting of expiated guilt, conscience set free banters itself with the torments it has undergone.

Never has an art offered the world anything so serene as these symphonies in A and F major, and all those works so intimately related to them which the master produced during the divine period of his total deafness. Their effect upon the hearer is that of setting him free from the sense of guilt, just as their after-effect is a feeling of "paradise lost", with which one again turns towards the world of phenomena. Thus these wonderful works preach repentance and atonement in the deepest sense of a divine revelation.

The aesthetic idea of the *Sublime* is alone applicable here: for the effect of serenity passes at once far beyond any satisfaction to be derived from mere beauty. The defiance of reason, proud in its powers of cognition, is wrecked upon the charm that subdues our entire nature: cognition flees, confessing its error, and in the immense joy over this confession we exult from the depth of our soul; no matter how seriously the fettered

72

mien of the listener may betray astonishment at the insufficiency of human sight and thought in the presence of this most veritable world.

What could the world see and realize of the human nature of the genius thus raised above and beyond the world? What could the eye of a man of the world perceive of him? Assuredly nothing but what was easily misunderstood, just as he himself misunderstood the world in his dealings with it; for to his simple great heart there was continuous contradiction in the world—that he could only resolve harmoniously in the sublime fields of art.

As far as his reason sought to comprehend the world, his mind was soothed with optimistic views, such as the visionary enthusiasm of the last century's humanitarian tendencies had developed into a creed held in common by the middle-class religious world.

Every feeling of doubt, which experience of life aroused against the correctness of that doctrine, he fought against by loudly asserting fundamental religious maxims. His innermost self said to him: Love is God; and accordingly he too decreed: God is Love. Whatever touched upon these dogmas with any emphasis in the writings of our poets met with his approbation. "Faust" always had the strongest hold of him; yet he held Klopstock, and many a weaker bard of Humanitarianism, worthy of special veneration. His morality was of the strictest domestic exclusiveness: a frivolous mood put him in a rage. He certainly did not display, even to the most attentive observer, a single

trait of wit; and, in spite of Bettina's sentimental fan-
cies about Beethoven, Goethe probably had a hard time
in his conversations with him. But the same sure instinct which, as he felt no need of luxury, led him to be
frugal and watch his income to the verge of parsimony,
was also shown in his strict religious morality, and by
virtue of it he preserved his noblest treasure, the freedom of his genius, from the subjugation by the sur-
rounding world.

He lived in Vienna and knew Vienna only: that tells
its own tale.

The Austrians, who after the eradication of every
trace of German Protestantism, were educated in the
schools of Roman Jesuits, had even lost the correct pronunciation of their language; which like the classical
names of Antiquity, were pronounced to them in an
un-German Italianized fashion. German spirit, German
habits and ways, were explained from text-books of
Spanish and Italian origin! A people, joyous and gay
by nature, had been drilled on the basis of falsified history, falsified science, falsified religion, into a species
of scepticism, calculated to undermine all clinging to
the true, the genuine, and the free; a scepticism that in
the end appeared as downright frivolity.

Now it was this spirit which had imparted to music,
the only art cultivated in Austria, the direction and the
verily degrading tendency we have already commented
upon. We have seen how Beethoven's mighty nature
protected him from this tendency, and we may now
recognize in him a similar power to aid us energetically

in warding off frivolity in life and mind. Baptized and brought up as a Catholic, the entire spirit of German Protestantism lived in his disposition. And that spirit also led him as an artist into the path where he was to meet the only colleague in his art, before whom he might bow reverentially, and whom he could greet as a revelation of the profoundest mystery of his own nature. If Haydn passed for the teacher of his youth, the great *Sebastian Bach* became a guide for the man in the mighty development of his artistic life.

Bach's wondrous work became the Bible of his faith; he read in it, and forgot the world of sounds, which he heard no longer. There he found the enigma of his profoundest dream, which the poor Leipzig precentor had once written down as the eternal symbol of another and a new world. These were the same enigmatically entwined lines and marvellously intricate characters, in which the secret of the world and its shapes had been seen in the sheen of light by the great *Albrecht Dürer;* the charmed book of the necromancer who illumines the microcosm with the light of the macrocosm. What only the eye of the German spirit could behold, and *its* ear only could hear, what, from inmost perception, forced that spirit to irresistible protestation against alien things, *that* Beethoven read clearly and distinctly in its saintliest books, and—became himself a saint.

But how, again, in actual life, would such a saint stand with regard to his own sanctity, seeing that he was indeed enlightened "to speak the highest wisdom, but in a language which his reason did not understand"?

Must not his intercourse with the world resemble the condition of one who, awakening from deepest sleep, in vain endeavors to recall his blissful dream? We may assume a similar condition to obtain in the religious Saint, when, driven by dire necessity, he applies himself in some degree to the affairs of common life; only, in the very distress of life, a saint of religion clearly recognizes the atonement for a sinful existence, and, in the patient endurance of sad distress, he enthusiastically grasps the means of redemption; whilst *that* sainted Seer accepts the sense of an atonement as though it simply meant the endurance of pain, and pays the debt of existence solely as a sufferer. And the error of the optimist is thereupon revenged by enhanced sensitiveness, and a corresponding increase of suffering. Every want of feeling, every instance of selfishness or hardness of heart, such as he meets with again and again, incense him as an incomprehensible corruption of that original goodness of man to which he clings with religious faith. Thus he continually falls from the paradise of his inner harmony into a hell of fearfully discordant existence, and this discord again he can only resolve harmoniously as an artist.

If we wish to picture to ourselves a day in the life of our Saint, one of the master's own wonderful pieces may serve as a counterpart. Only, to avoid deceiving ourselves, we shall have to adhere strictly to the mode of procedure by which we analogically applied the phenomena of dreams to throw light upon the origin of music, without ever identifying the one with the other. I shall choose, then, to illustrate such a genuine "Beethoven day" by the light of its inmost occurrences, his great *string-quartet in C-sharp minor:* [opus 131] premising that if we rest content to recall the tone-poem to memory, an illustration of the sort may perhaps prove possible, at least up to a certain degree; whereas it would hardly be feasible during an actual performance. For, whilst listening to the work, we are bound to eschew any definite comparisons, being solely conscious of an immediate revelation from another world. Even then, however, the animation of the picture in its several details has to be left to the reader's fancy, and an outline sketch must therefore suffice.

The long introductory *Adagio,* than which probably nothing more melancholy has been expressed in tones, I would designate as the awakening on the morn of a day that throughout its tardy course shall fullfil not a single desire: not one.* None the less it is a penitential prayer, a conference with God in the faith of the eternally good. The eye turned inwards here, too, sees the comforting phenomena it alone can perceive (Allegro $\frac{6}{8}$), in which the longing becomes a sweet, tender, melancholy disport with itself, the inmost hidden dream-picture awakens as the loveliest reminiscence. And now, in the short transitional *Allegro Moderato,* it is as though the master, conscious of his strength, puts him-

* A paraphrase, probably intentional, of lines spoken by Faust in the fourth scene of Goethe's play.—Ed.

self in position to work his spells; with renewed power he now practices his magic (Andante $\frac{2}{4}$) in banning a lovely figure, the witness of pure heavenly innocence, so that he may incessantly enrapture himself by its ever new and unheard-of transformations, induced by the refraction of the rays of light he casts upon it.

We may now (Presto $\frac{2}{2}$) fancy him, profoundly happy from within, casting an inexpressibly serene glance upon the outer world, and, again, it stands before him as in the Pastoral Symphony. Everything is luminous, reflecting his inner happiness. It is as though he were listening to the very tones emitted by the phenomena, that move, aerial and again firm, in a rhythmical dance before him. He contemplates Life, and appears to reflect how he is to play a dance for Life itself; (Short Adagio $\frac{3}{4}$) a short but troubled meditation—as though he were diving into the deep dream of his soul. He has again caught sight of the inner side of the world; he wakens, and strikes the strings for a dance, such as the world has never heard (Allegro Finale). It is the World's own dance: wild delight, cries of anguish, love's ecstasy, highest rapture, misery, rage; voluptuous now, and sorrowful; lightning's quiver, storm's roll; and high above the gigantic musician! banning and compelling all things, proudly and firmly wielding them from whirl to whirlpool, to the abyss.—He laughs at himself; for the incantation was, after all, but play to him. Thus night beckons. His day is done.

It is not possible to consider the man, Beethoven, in

any sort of light, without at once having recourse to the wonderful musician by way of elucidation.

We noted how the instinctive tendency of his life coincided with a tendency towards the emancipation of his art; he could not be a servant of luxury, and his music had to be cleared of all traces of subordination to a frivolous taste. Moreover, as to the way in which his optimistic religious faith went hand in hand with the instinctive proclivity towards widening the sphere of his art, we have testimony of the noblest simplicity in the *Choral Symphony,* the genesis of which it now behoves us to consider more closely, so as to throw light upon the wonderful connection between the designated fundamental tendencies in the nature of our Saint.

The identical impulse which led Beethoven's reason to construct the Idea of the Good Man, guided him in the quest of the *melody* proper to this Good Man. He wished to restore to melody that purity which it had lost in the hands of trained musicians. One has but to recall the Italian operatic melody of the last century, to perceive how curiously vapid a tone specter, exclusively devoted to fashion and its ends, that melody was. By it, and through its use, music had become deeply degraded, so that men's eager taste constantly hankered after some new tune, as the tune of yesterday was no longer fit to be heard to-day. Yet, in the main, instrumental music, too, drew its sustenance from that sort of melody; and we have already seen how it was made use of for the ends of a social life, anything rather than noble.

79

Haydn forthwith took up the sturdy and jolly dance-tunes of the people, which, as is sufficiently obvious, he often appropriated from the dances of the neighboring Hungarian peasants. So far he remained in a lower sphere, closely confined within the limits of its local character. But from what sphere was melody to be taken, if it was to bear a noble, enduring character? For those peasants' dance-tunes of Haydn's were chiefly attractive as piquant oddities; they could not be expected to form a purely human art-type, valid for all times. Yet it was impossible to derive such melody from the higher sphere of society, for that sphere was ruled by the vicious, cockered, curlicued melody of the opera-singer and ballet-dancer.

Beethoven, too, took Haydn's course, only he was no longer content to treat popular dance-tunes so as to furnish entertainment at a princely table, but he played them, in an ideal sense, to the people themselves. It was now a Scotch, then a Russian, or an Old French people's-tune, in which he recognised that nobility of innocence he dreamt of, and at whose feet he did homage with his whole art. And with an Hungarian peasant's dance he played (in the last movement of his A-major symphony) a tune to all nature, so that whoever should see her dancing to it might deem he saw a new planet before his very eyes in the prodigious circling vortex.*

* Massine's choreographic treatment of this symphony is not greatly different from this, though he associates the evolution of the universe with the first, rather than the last, movement.—Ed.

On Beethoven

But the problem was to find the arch-type of purity, the "good man," and to wed him to his "God is love."

One might trace the master upon this track already in his "Eroica" symphony: it is as though he meant to use the uncommonly simple theme of the last movement, which he also carried out elsewhere, as the groundwork for this purpose; but, whatever of transporting *Melos* he built upon that theme, belongs rather too much to the sentimental Mozartian *cantabile,* which he expanded and developed in such a peculiar way, to serve as a type of an achievement in the sense intended.

The trace is more distinct in the jubilant final movement of the C-minor symphony, in which the simple march melody, based almost entirely upon tonic and dominant and the natural notes of horns and trumpets, moves us so much the more by its grand simplicity, as the preceding symphony now appears as a protracted preparation, holding us in suspense, like clouds, moved now by storms, now by delicate breezes, from which at length the sun bursts forth in full splendor.

But the C-minor symphony (we introduce this apparent digression as important to the subject) engages our attention as one of the rarer conceptions of the master in which, from a ground of painful agitation, passion soars upwards on a scale of consolation, exultation, to a final outburst of consciously triumphant joy. Here the lyric pathos almost touches upon an ideal dramatic sphere; and, whilst it may appear dubious whether the purity of musical conception might not thus be impaired—as it must lead to the introduction of ideas which seem quite alien to the spirit of music—it should, on the other hand not be overlooked that the master was by no means led thither by any aberration of aesthetical speculation, but solely by an instinct, altogether ideal, which germinated in the true domain of music.

This instinct coincided, as we have shown at the outset of this latter investigation, with an effort to rescue the faith in the primitive goodness of man, or perhaps to regain it, in the face of all protests of experience that might be referred to mere delusion. Those conceptions of the master's which originated mainly in the spirit of sublime serenity, belonged, as we saw above, for the most part to that period of his beatific isolation which, after complete deafness had set in, seems to have entirely removed him from the world of suffering. There is, perhaps, no need to assume a decline of that inner serenity on the ground of the more painful mood, which now appears in certain of Beethoven's most important conceptions; for we should assuredly err were we to believe that an artist can ever conceive save in deep serenity of soul. The mood expressed by the conception must therefore pertain to the idea of the world itself, which the artist apprehends, and interprets in the work of art. But then, as we positively assumed that an *Idea of the world* is revealed in music, so the conceiving musician must above all be taken as himself included in that Idea; and what he utters is not *his view* of the world, but rather the world itself, wherein weal and woe, grief and joy alternate.

By Peter Tchaikovsky

To begin with Beethoven, whom I praise uncondi-
tionally, and to whom I bend as to a god.* But what is
Beethoven to me? I bow down before the grandeur of
some of his creations, but I do not love Beethoven. My
relationship to him reminds me of that which I felt in
my childhood to the God Jehovah. I feel for him—for
my sentiments are still unchanged—great veneration,
but also fear. He has created the heaven and the earth,
and although I fall down before him, I do not love
him. Christ, on the contrary, calls forth exclusively the
feeling of *love*. He is God, but also Man. He has suffered like ourselves. We pity Him and love in Him the
ideal side of man's nature. If Beethoven holds an analogous place in my heart to the God Jehovah, I love
Mozart as the musical Christ. I do not think this comparison is blasphemous. Mozart was as pure as an angel, and his music is full of divine beauty.

* An excerpt from Tchaikovsky's diary, 1886.

Tchaikovsky

While speaking of Beethoven I touch on Mozart. To my mind, Mozart is the culminating point of all beauty in the sphere of music. He alone can make me weep and tremble with delight at the consciousness of the approach of that which we call the ideal. Beethoven makes me tremble too, but rather from a sense of fear and yearning anguish. I do not understand how to analyze music, and cannot go into detail. . . . Still I must mention two facts. I love Beethoven's middle period, and sometimes his first; but I really hate his *last,* especially the latest quartets. They have only brilliancy, nothing more. The rest is chaos, over which floats, veiled in mist, the spirit of this musical Jehovah.

I love everything in Mozart, for we love everything in the man to whom we are truly devoted. Above all, *Don Juan,* for through that work I have learnt to know what music is. Till then (my seventeenth year) I knew nothing except the enjoyable *semi-music* of the Italians. Although I love everything in Mozart, I will not assert that every one of his works, even the most insignificant, should be considered a masterpiece. I know quite well that no single example of his Sonatas is a great creation, and yet I like each one, because it is his, because he has breathed into it his sacred breath.

As to the forerunner of both these artists, I like to play Bach, because it is interesting to play a good fugue; but I do not regard him, in common with many others, as a great genius. Handel is only fourth-rate, he is not even interesting. I sympathize with Gluck in spite of his poor creative gift.* I also like some things of Haydn. These four great masters have been surpassed by Mozart. They are rays which are extinguished by Mozart's sun.

* A gracious gesture!—Ed.

By Hugo Wolf

Two whispering neighbors seated behind me man-
aged, by their inconsiderate behavior, to deprive me of
all enjoyment of the overture.* "Lackey-souls" is what
Kreisler, the conductor, once termed these disturbers of
the peace, these creatures who whisper while the music
is played, rattle their fans, stare stupidly around them,
greet their acquaintances, wave to their friends, slam
their seats, snap their opera-glass cases open and shut,
keep time to the music with their stamping feet, or drum
out the tempo with their fingers, and perform countless
other stupidities.) One of these lackey-souls (what a
wonderfully fitting phrase) behind me turned to his fellow lackey-soul to pronounce the following memorable
words—while the great *Leonora Overture* was being
played: "Just look! The audience is as attentive as if it
were at a concert!"

* This article was written apropos a performance of *Fidelio*
in Vienna with Sucher and Vogl in June 1884.

86

I was overwhelmed by this bit of unblushing naïveté. There it was—at last. The natural and obvious behavior of a civilized audience considered curious and abnormal, even though a Zulu Island native could not be anything but absolutely quiet and attentive once the first notes of the overture filled the hall!

Is it any the less music if it is played in a theater instead of a concert hall? Does the quality of the music depend upon the room in which it is played? What hair-raising nonsense! Do Mozart, Wagner and Gluck cease to be music once they are heard in an opera? Are the great pieces of these masters to be used as mere incidents to the tableaux, for the benefit of those bored, dirty, loose lackey-souls who flitter from box to box, and loge to loge? Truly a dishonorable role for the Muse of our composers—to be riding pack-mules and camels. It is enough to turn a dove into a tiger to see the abandonment of the true, pure and only Muse of our dramatic composers, Gluck, Mozart, Weber, Marschner, and Wagner, to the cold scorn and disdainful stupidity of those who betray their lackey-souls in theaters and concert halls.

What is to be inferred from the above-quoted words of my dear neighbors? That one attends the opera to hear music? Heavens, no—anything but that! Even the best, most sensitive, most thoughtful of these lackey-souls attends the opera only to feed upon the striking scenery, the luscious hips of the ballerina, or the pretty voice of a singer. They have an eye for everything that is insignificant and unimportant. Everything is sympa-

87

thetically observed but the music. For that they have only a cold and menacing attitude. And these are the best of the lot! Second to them are those theater-goers who attend the opera only to observe Society, fashions, and the latest coiffures, all of which are best visible during the prelude and certain well-lighted scenes.* These people maintain a shatter-proof indifference to even the most sensational and colorful events on the stage. Singers are unimportant. For them the chief role in the opera is played by the virtuosos of opera-glass twirling and handling.

But bad as they are, these lackey-souls are not the worst—the ultimate in the whole category of the species is achieved by those who attend the opera for no other reason than to let themselves be seen. They come regularly only after the last notes of the overture fade away, as noisy in their entrance as poorly mannered children, slamming their seats and snapping their inevitable opera-glass cases open with as much noise as possible before beginning to talk. The conversation is usually lively, and beneath the gaiety and laughter a distinct undertone of business is discerned. "It's going up," "it's going down" are as frequently heard and exchanged in their talk as Piano and Forte in the orchestra. Figures are sprayed throughout the words, etc.,

* Wolf's outburst is merely a confirmation—if one compares the comments of Berlioz on the Paris audience or those of Newman on the Metropolitan's public—of the opinion that it is the surroundings rather than the city that determine behaviour.

etc., and if ladies are along family matters, too, are not omitted. The cook has a novel way of preparing roast goose; the children are growing up to be *so* talented, clever, and promising. Elsie, the little 5 year old, can already play all of Mendelssohn's "Songs without Words" by heart! And little Sigismund, or it may be Siegfried, is writing poetry——.

"Too much," I say, agreeing with Tannhäuser, "it's too much."

On Mozart

By Charles Gounod

A vacation of several days arrived (that of the New Year), of which my mother took advantage to procure for me a pleasure that was at the same time a great and impressive lesson.* They were giving Mozart's *Don Giovanni,* at the *Italiens,* to a hearing of which she took me herself; and that heavenly evening spent with her in a little box on the fourth floor of that theater is one of the most memorable and delightful of my life. I cannot say if my memory is correct, but I think it was Reicha who advised her to take me to hear *Don Giovanni.*

Before describing the emotion produced in me by that incomparable *chef-d'oeuvre,* I ask myself if my pen can ever transcribe it—I do not say faithfully, as that would be impossible—but at least in a manner to

* This excerpt from Gounod's *Mémoires* concerns an impression of, approximately, his eighteenth year—1836—when he was a student at the Conservatoire.

give some idea of what went on in my mind during those few hours, the charm of which has dominated my life like a luminous apparition, or a kind of vision of revelation.

From the very beginning of the overture I felt myself transported into an absolutely new world, by the solemn and majestic chords of the final scene of the Commandant. I was seized with a freezing terror; and when came the threatening progression over which are unrolled those ascending and descending scales, fatal and inexorable as a sentence of death, I was overcome with such a fright that I hid my face upon my mother's shoulder, and thus enveloped in the double embrace of the beautiful and the terrible, I murmured the following words:

"Oh! Mamma, what music! that is, indeed, real music!"

The hearing of Rossini's *Othello* stirred in me the fibers of musical instinct, but the effect produced by *Don Juan* had quite another significance, and an entirely different result. It seemed to me that between these two kinds of impressions there must be something analogous to that felt by a painter in passing directly from contact with the Venetian masters to that with Raphael, Leonardo da Vinci, and Michelangelo. Rossini gave me to know the intoxication of purely musical delight; he charmed me, delighted my ear. Mozart did more; to that enjoyment so complete, from an exclusively musical and emotional point of view, was then added the profound and penetrating influence of true expression united to perfect beauty.

It was, from one end to the other of the score, a long and inexpressible delight. The pathetic tones of the trio at the death of the Commandant, and of Donna Anna's lament over the body of her father, the charming grace of Zerlina, the supreme and stately elegance of the trio of the Masks, and of that which begins the second act under Donna Elvira's window—all, finally (for in this immortal work all must be mentioned), created for me that beatitude one feels only in the presence of the essentially beautiful things that hold the admiration of the centuries, and serve to fix the height of the esthetic level of perfection in art.

This representation counts as one of the most cherished holiday gifts of my childhood, and later, when I had won the *prix de Rome* it was the full score of *Don Juan* that my dear mother gave me as a reward.

ON THE PERFORMANCE OF MOZART

Mozart's music, so clear, true, natural, and penetrating, is, notwithstanding, seldom perfectly performed.*

What is the reason?

This is the question I propose to examine, and, if possible, to make comprehensible to my readers. In the execution of the works of Mozart, it is necessary, before

* Apropos the hundredth anniversary of the first performance of *Don Giovanni* in Prague in 1787, Gounod wrote a commentary on the score, of which this is the final section.

everything, to avoid *seeking for effect*. I mean here by
the word *effect*, not the impression produced on the listener by the work itself, an impression of charm, grace,
tenderness, terror—in a word, all the feelings which
the musical text offers, or, at least, should offer, *by itself* in the form and portrayal—but that *exaggeration*
of accent, light and shade, and time which too often
leads the executants to substitute their own ideas for
those of the author, and to distort the nature of his
thoughts instead of reproducing them simply and faithfully. When a great musician has written a work, and
such a musician as Mozart, the least that one can do
him the honor to suppose is that he has *wished* to
write *what* he has written, and there are very strong
presumptive reasons for saying that in trying to express
more than Mozart has done they would express *less*.

What would be thought of an engraver who should
replace by outlines and figures of his own those of a
picture by Raphael?

Does an actor dare to introduce a phrase, a verse, a
word of his own invention in a work of Racine or
Molière?

Why should the language of *sounds* be treated with
less respect than that of words?

Is the truth of expression less an obligation in one
than the other?

What remains of a musical thought if executants distort accents, nuances, and the respective values of notes?
Absolutely nothing. Many singers do not give the least
thought to these matters. Preoccupied as they too often

are with the idea of gaining admiration for their voices, they sacrifice without scruple *the demands of expression to the success of the virtuoso,* and the lasting triumph of truth to the empty and evanescent gratification of vanity.*

It is hardly necessary to say that in thus permitting personal whims to replace obedience to the text, a gulf is created between the author and the auditor. What meaning is there, for example, in a prolonged pause on certain notes, to the detriment of the rhythm and the balance of the musical phrase? Do they reflect for an instant on the perpetual irritation caused to the listener—to say nothing of the insupportable monotony of the proceeding itself? And then what becomes of the orchestral design in this constant subordination to the singer's caprice? It is impossible to draw up a complete catalogue of abuses and licenses of all sorts which in the execution alter the nature of the sense, and compromise the impression of a musical phrase.

One may be permitted to remind musicians that want of attention to the following points causes nearly all the infractions of the rules of art and of good taste:

> The rate of movement.
> The light and shade.
> The breathing.
> The pronunciation.
> The conductor.

* One wonders, in the light of this, what Gounod would have thought of the way in which *Faust* is customarily given these days!—Ed.

On Mozart

I.—*The Rate of Movement*

Whenever the real expression, the true character, the just sentiment of a piece depends upon the ensemble, the most important, the most indispensable condition is, undoubtedly, the exact and scrupulous observance of the time in which the composer has conceived it. The speed determines its general *character,* and, as this *character* is an essential part of the idea, to alter the time is to alter the idea itself to such a degree as to destroy sometimes the sense and expression.

It cannot be denied that a musical phrase may be absolutely travestied and disfigured by an excess of slowness or rapidity of the time in which it is performed. I could quote many examples. Here is one which I shall never forget, it shocked me so much. At a ball given by the Minister of State during the winter of 1854–55, if I mistake not, the old *contredanse* (quadrille) was still in existence, or rather, was just dying out. All of a sudden I heard the orchestra strike up the first figure. Horror! abomination! sacrilege! It was the sublime air of the High Priest of Isis in Mozart's "Il Flauto Magico" falling from the height of its solemn and sacred rhythm into the grotesque stamping of satin shoes and patent leather boots. I fled as if I had the devil at my heels!

However, a very incomplete idea of the importance of the musical movement would be formed if it were considered purely from a mathematical point of view only, and I shall now endeavor to consider the circumstances which might cause mathematical differences in the time, the music nevertheless retaining its identity of character and expression.

1st. The size of the building in which the performance is held. This is a question of acoustics and proportion. In a very large hall, a movement would bear to be taken less quickly than if executed in a smaller one.

2nd. The style of the executant, and the amplitude of delivery, and the production of the voice.

I will cite here two famous examples—Duprez and Faure. When Duprez came to the Opera and filled the place which Nourrit had occupied with so much brilliancy and distinction for fifteen years, it was a complete revolution in lyrical declamation. Nourrit was a great artist; the dignity of his character, the culture of his intelligence, a constant care of truth in his varied and numerous roles of the répertoire of that period— these qualities obtained for him not only the favor and esteem of the public, but an influence at the theater which was felt by all around him. With rare talent as an artist he played the principal parts in all the grand operas, from "La Vestale," "Masaniello," and "Guillaume Tell," to "Robert le Diable," "La Juive" and the "Les Huguenots," in the last of which he created the part of Raoul de Nangis, stamping it with an ineffaceable impression. His powerful acting so held his audience, that he succeeded in making them forget that his voice was a little thin and guttural, and that he used the falsetto register too frequently. The coming of Duprez took everybody by storm. I was present at his début, which took place in the part of Arnold ("Guillaume Tell"). Duprez returned from Italy preceded by a great reputation and the well known story of the chest C, which was to raise a tempest of applause at the end of the celebrated air of the last act. It was unnecessary to wait till then to know that the success of the great singer was assured. In two bars it was made. From the first verse of the recitative, "Il me parle d'hymen! Jamais, jamais le mien!" one felt that this was a transformation in the art of singing, and when Duprez finished the phrase of the duet in the second act "Oh, Mathilde! idole de mon âme," there was a frenzy of enthusiasm throughout the house. He had a breadth of declamation and volume of tone which captivated the hearer, and the admirable melodies of the great Italian master shone with a new luster owing to the marvelous notes of his voice. The use of the chest voice and the amplitude of his declamation permitted Duprez to take the time slower than his illustrious predecessor had done without appearing to alter it, so well did he know how to captivate the ear by the fullness of his voice, and to move the audience by his dramatic powers.

Faure in our day has been a new and striking example of the same thing. He produces the sounds with such richness and fullness, he gives them such interest by a continual modulation of the tone (and occasionally, perhaps, a little more than is necessary), that one forgets the duration which he gives them, and which is hidden under his admirable method and his unrivalled pronunciation. To these illustrious names must be added those of Pauline Viardot, Miolan Carvalho, Gabrielle Krauss, the brothers De Reszke, Lassalle, and others who have understood the importance of declamation. But the preceding remarks on time have nothing to do with the accent, which is also, from an entirely different point of view, a matter of great importance. Unfortunately, many singers of today do not sufficiently consider this subject, great detriment being caused to the music and considerable annoyance to both composer and conductor.

Much might be said upon this topic. I must be satisfied to touch lightly upon it, as this is not the place to set forth a complete course of musical education.

II.—*The Bar (La Mésure)*

Disregard of the accent is one of the modern faults, for it entirely destroys the musical equilibrium. Many singers regard the bar as an insupportable yoke, and as an obstacle to feeling and expression. They think that it makes machines of them, and that it takes away all grace, charm, warmth, and freedom in performance. Now it is exactly the reverse. The bar, instead of being the enemy to the musical phrase, gives protection and freedom to it. It is not difficult to demonstrate this. Let us consider it first as a principle of unanimity of performance. The essential character of the bar is the equality of the duration of the beats which compose it. If, then, inequality is introduced, the unity which is essential to the phrase, and which alone permits one to feel it, is destroyed.

2nd. If the misrepresentation of the bar is injurious to such an extent upon an isolated phrase, what confusion will it not bring in the execution of an ensemble? The effect would be indescribable.

3rd. There is still the orchestra to be considered. It presents a multitude of figures of accompaniment subjected to the laws of accent, and from which laws there can be no deviation under penalty of abominable confusion. Sixty or eighty musicians cannot be left in a state of constant uncertainty. Deprived of the word of command, they will not know what to do in order to avoid disorder and cacophony.

But the bar, which is a principle of order with regard to the rhythm, is no less essential to the expression. The idea of the bar includes that of rhythm, which is its characteristic sub-division.

To neglect the bar and its regulating influence injures the rhythm and the prosody.

These few reflections are sufficient to give an idea of the detrimental effects which disregard of the accent may cause to musical works. Another question of extreme importance in the matter of musical expression is that of light and shade.

* * *

III.—*The Nuances*

We understand by the word "nuance" the degree of intensity of any sound, whether it be produced by a voice or instrument. That is to say, the gradations of tone play in musical art a part analogous to that of proportion in the art of painting.

We see by this how the true observation of the nuances is indispensable to the faithful rendering of a musical phrase, and to what degree the thoughtless caprice of the executant can alter the sense and character to such an extent as to make it unrecognizable by substituting for the author's intentions and indications the nuances and accents of pure fancy. It is here that the independence of the singer most frequently finds the opportunity of giving free scope to his imagination, and Heaven knows how he uses it.

It matters little whether the accent be neglected, whether the prosody be sacrificed, whether the melodic figure be altered, or whether affectation destroys the logical and natural movement of the musical phrase, provided that the *sound* be noticed and applauded for *itself*. These performers are entirely mistaken as to the function and role of the *voice*. They take the *means* for the *end* and the servant for the master. They forget that fundamentally there is but one art, the *word*, and one function, *to express,* and that consequently a great singer ought to be first of all a great *orator*, and that is utterly impossible without absolutely truthful accent. When singers, especially on the stage, think only of displaying the voice, they should be reminded that that is a sure and infallible means of falling into monotony; truth alone has the privilege of infinite and inexhaustible variety.

On Mozart

IV.—*The Breathing*

This important question of the breathing may be regarded under two distinct aspects—the one purely expressive. Under the first it devolves upon the composer to write in such a way as not to exceed the power of the respiratory organs, under the penalty of seeing his musical phrase divided into fragments, which would disfigure it. But as regards the expression, it is another thing. Here it is prosody and punctuation which determine and regulate the expression. Unfortunately this rule is seldom observed. A singer does not scruple to divide a section of a phrase, often even a word, in order to take breath, for the sake of a sound to which they wish to give exaggerated power and duration, to the detriment of the musical sense and the prosody, which ought to be the first consideration. It is ridiculous to introduce, for example, a respiration between "my" and "love" in the phrase

"To thee I give my love"

—a respiration which nothing can justify; but then the singer has had the pleasure of showing off on a short syllable until all the breath has been used, just for the sake of gaining a noisy demonstration of conventional applause. Such licenses simply disfigure the form of the musical idea, and are revolting to common sense.

101

V.—*The Pronunciation*

There are two special points to observe in the pronunciation.

1st. It should be clear, neat, distinct, exact; that is to say, the ear ought not to be left in any uncertainty as to the word pronounced.

2nd. It should be expressive, that is to say, *to paint in the mind the feeling* enunciated by the word itself. All that concerns clearness, neatness, and exactness may be more properly classed as *articulation*. Articulation relates to the due formation of every sound in the word. Everything else may be described as *pronunciation*. It is by the latter that we make the word picture the thought, the feeling, the passion which it envelops. In short, the function of articulation is to form the material sounds of a word, whereas that of pronunciation is to reveal its inner meaning. Articulation gives clearness to the word; pronunciation gives it eloquence. True instinct, though lacking culture, can make all these distinctions apparent. One cannot insist too much upon the value and interest which clear articulation and expressive pronunciation give to singing, so important are they. By the force of expression, they exercise such a power over the listener that they make him forget the insufficiency or the mediocrity of the vocal organ; whilst the absence of these qualities, though the voice may be the most beautiful in the world, leaves him unmoved.

The foregoing considerations show how much depends upon simplicity, sincerity, and freedom from all preoccupation as to personal success.

Can there be a higher ambition for a performer than to be an artist capable and worthy of interpreting Mozart's music, so pure and so true; or a more noble dream than to inspire love for the works of such a master, and thus contribute to the sacred and salutary devotion to the true and the beautiful? But, alas, in art, as in everything else, the abnegation of self is rare, although it is the condition of all true greatness.

VI.—*The Conductor*

The conductor is the *center* of the musical performance. This word, in itself, shows the importance and responsibility of his functions.

First of all, the unity of the movement, without which there is no possible ensemble, is in the hands of the conductor. That is self-evident, and does not need demonstration. It is on this point most necessary, and at the same time most easy, for the conductor to make his authority felt; his baton is one of command.

But, apart from the ensembles, how often does this command degenerate into servitude? What compliance there is to the caprices of the singers, and what fatal neglect of the interests of art and the real value of the works performed!

However, it is not necessary that the rule of the conductor should amount to an unyielding and mechanical rigidity, which would be the absurd triumph of the *letter* over the *spirit*.

A conductor who would be like an inflexible metronome throughout a musical composition would be guilty of an excess of strictness as unbearable as an excess of laxity.

The great art of the conductor is that power which may be called suggestive, and which elicits from the singer an unconscious obedience, whilst making him believe that it is his own will that he follows. In short, the singer must be persuaded and not constrained. Power is not in the will, but in the intelligence; it is not questioned, but it is felt. It behoves the conductor then, to understand, and to make others understand how much he will concede to them in the matter of time without altering the character of the movement. It is his duty to seize upon the difference between elasticity and stiffness, and to atone, without abruptness, for any momentary retardation by an imperceptible return to the normal and regular time.

It is also essential that the conductor should not mistake precipitation for warr 'h—the result would be to sacrifice the rhythmical power of the declamation and the fulness of tone. It is commonly imagined that a *crescendo* ought to be *hurried,* and a *diminuendo* gradually slackened. Now, it is precisely the contrary which is nearly always the case. It stands to reason that one feels inclined to lengthen a sound in augmenting its intensity, and vice versa. But this is not all.

It is an error to think that the conductor can make

himself entirely understood by means of the baton or the bow which he holds in his hand. His whole demeanor should instruct and animate those who obey him. His attitude, his physiognomy, his glance should prepare the singers for that which is demanded of them; his expression should cause them to anticipate his intentions, and should enlighten the executants.

Yet it is not necessary for him to indulge in wild gesticulations. True power is calm, and when the poet of antiquity wished to express the might of Jupiter, he represented him as making the whole of Olympus tremble at his nod. In short, the conductor is the ambassador of the master's Thought; he is responsible for it to the artists and to the public, and *ought to be* the living expression, the faithful mirror, the incorruptible depositary of it. One could write volumes upon the important duties of a conductor, and I certainly hold that these duties should be made the object of a regular course of lectures, the plan for which might be clearly indicated in the general musical education given by our conservatoires. Here is a want which I hope may be supplied in the future. Besides the considerable benefit which would accrue to the musical works, this would be an opening offered to a whole group of special aptitudes, which are as rare as they are necessary; it would also be a serious guarantee of authority to the artists.

Gluck on His Own System

When I undertook to set the opera of 'Alceste' to music I proposed to myself to avoid all the abuses that the mistaken vanity of singers and the excessive complaisance of composers had introduced into Italian opera, and which had converted the most stately and beautiful of all spectacles into one of the most tiresome and ridiculous.* I sought to confine the music to its true function, that of assisting the poetry, by strengthening both the expression of the sentiments and the interest of the situations; and this without either interrupting the action or chilling it by the introduction of superfluous ornaments. I thought that music should add to the poetry precisely what is added to a correct and well conceived drawing, when the

* This so-called 'manifesto' of a new order in operatic composition was published as a preface to *Alceste* 1767. Certainly Gluck was faithful to its tenets, but it can hardly be said that its effect was universal.—Ed.

vivacity of the colors and the happy harmony of light and shade serve to animate the figures, without changing their outline.

I have taken particular care not to interrupt an actor, in the warmth of dialogue, in order to make him wait for the end of a ritornello; or to stop him in the middle of his discourse upon a favourable vowel; either for the purpose of providing a long passage for the display of his beautiful voice, or, in order that he should wait for the orchestra to give him time to take breath for a cadence. I have not thought it necessary to pass rapidly over the second part of an air, although it might be one of the most passionate and important; and finish the air, notwithstanding that there is no conclusion in the sense, merely to give the singer an opportunity of showing his capability, by capriciously rendering a passage in different ways. In short, I have tried to banish all these abuses, against which good sense and reason have protested so long in vain.

I have imagined that the overture should warn the spectators of the character of the action to be submitted to them, as well as indicate its subject; and that the instruments should only be requisitioned in proportion to the degree of interest or passion; and that it was necessary to avoid, in the dialogue, too violent a distinction between the air and the recitative; to secure that the period should not be marked off abruptly, in interruption of the sense; and that the movement and the warmth of the scene should not be inappropriately intruded upon. My belief has also been that the work should, above all things, aim at a beautiful simplicity; and I have thus avoided all parade of difficulties, at the expense of clearness. I have not attached the least value to the discovery of a novelty, unless naturally suggested by the situation and wedded to its expression. Finally, there is no rule which I have not felt I ought willingly to sacrifice in favor of effect.

On Bach

By Hector Berlioz

The day on which I went to the Singing Academy,* by the director's invitation, they performed Sebastian Bach's *Passion*. This famous score, which you have, no doubt, read, is written for two choruses and two orchestras. The singers, to the number of at least three hundred, were seated on the steps of a large amphitheater, exactly like the one we have in the chemistry lecture-room in the Jardin des Plantes; a space of only three or four feet separates the two choruses. The two orchestras, rather small ones, accompanied the voices from the upper steps, behind the choruses, and were thus pretty far from the *Kapellmeister*, who stood down in front beside the piano-forte. I should not have said piano-forte, but harpsichord; for it had almost the

* In Berlin. The letter from which this is extracted was written during Berlioz's visit to Germany in 1841–2, and addressed to his friend Desmarest, First 'cellist of the Conservatoire orchestra.—Ed.

tone of the wretched instruments of that name which were in use in Bach's time. I do not know whether they made such a choice designedly, but I noticed in the singing schools, in the green-rooms of the theaters, everywhere where voices were to be accompanied, that the piano-forte intended for that purpose was invariably the most detestable that could be found. The one Mendelssohn used in Leipzig in the hall of the Gewandhaus forms the sole exception.

You will ask me what the harpsichord-piano can have to do *during the performance* of a work in which the composer has not used this instrument! * It accompanies, together with the flutes, oboes, violins and basses, and probably serves to keep the first rows of the chorus up to pitch, as they *are supposed* not to hear, in the *tutti,* the orchestra, which is too far off. At any rate it is the custom. The continual tinkling of chords struck on this bad piano produces the most tiresome effect, and spreads over the ensemble a superfluous coating of monotony; but that is, no doubt, another reason for not giving it up. An old custom is so sacred, when it is a bad one!

The singers all remain seated during the pauses, and rise at the moment of singing. There is, I think, a real advantage in respect to a good emission of the voice in

* A curious oversight for a musician of Berlioz's vast information. Presumably the work he heard was the *St. Matthew Passion,* for which Mendelssohn was so ardent a propagandist. The cembalo is utilized here, of course, as an integral part of the musical structure.—Ed.

singing standing; it is only unfortunate that the chorus, giving up too easily to the fatigue of this posture, sit down as soon as their phrase is over; for in a work like Bach's, where the two answering choruses are often interrupted by solo recitative, it happens that there is always some group getting up or some sitting down, and in the long run this succession of movements up and down gets to be rather laughable; besides it takes away all the surprise from certain entries of the chorus, the eye notifying the ear beforehand from what part of the vocal body the sound is to come. I should rather have the chorus keep seated unless they can keep standing. But this impossibility is one of those that disappear immediately if the director knows how to say: *I wish it* or *I do not wish it.*

Be it as it may, the execution of those vocal masses was something imposing to me; the first *tutti* of the two choruses took away my breath; I was far from suspecting the power of that great harmonic blast. Yet we must recognize the fact that one gets tired of this beautiful sonority more quickly than of that of the orchestra, the qualities of the voice being less varied than those of the instruments. This is conceivable; there are hardly four voices of different natures, while the number of instruments of different kinds amounts to over thirty.

You do not expect of me, I fancy, my dear Desmarest, an analysis of Bach's great work; that would be wholly overstepping the limits I have had to impose upon myself. Besides the selection they played at the Conservatoire three years ago may be considered as

111

the type of the composer's style and manner in this work. The Germans profess an unlimited admiration for his recitatives, and their preeminent quality is precisely the one to have escaped me, as I do not understand the language in which they are written, and could not consequently appreciate the merit of their expression.

When one comes from Paris and knows our musical customs, one must witness the respect, the attention, the piety with which a German audience listens to such a composition, to believe it. Every one follows the words of the text with his eyes; not a movement in the house, not a murmur of approbation or blame, not the least applause; they are listening to a sermon, hearing the Gospel sung; they are attending in silence, not a concert but a divine service. And it is really thus that this music ought to be listened to. They adore Bach, and believe in him, without supposing for an instant that his divinity can ever be questioned; a heretic would horrify them; it is even forbidden to speak on the subject. Bach is Bach, as God is God.

On Chopin

By Robert Schumann

AN "OPUS 2"

Eusebius entered, not long ago.* You know his pale
face, and the ironical smile with which he awakens
expectation. I sat with Florestan at the pianoforte.
Florestan is, as you know, one of those rare musical
minds that foresee, as it were, coming, novel, or extraordinary things. But he encountered a surprise today. With the words, "Off with your hats, gentlemen,
—a genius!" Eusebius laid down a piece of music. We
were not allowed to see the title-page. I turned over
the leaves vacantly; the veiled enjoyment of music

* This celebrated essay, in which an appraisal of Chopin's
genius was first given to the world, was published in the
Allegemeine Musikalische Zeitung in 1831. It marks the first
appearance of Florestan and Eusebius, the names which Schumann gave to the two conflicting aspects of his own nature.
The first he visualized as representing the bold, impetuous
impulses of his character; the latter, the more contemplative,
fanciful tendencies.—Ed.

which one does not hear, has something magical in it. And besides this, every composer presents a different character of note-forms to the eye; Beethoven looks very different from Mozart, on paper; the difference resembles that between Jean Paul's and Goethe's prose.

But here it seemed as if eyes, strange to me, were glancing up at me,—flower eyes, basilisk eyes, peacock's eyes, maiden's eyes; in many places it looked yet brighter—I thought I saw Mozart's "La ci darem la mano" wound through a hundred chords, Leporello seemed to wink at me, and Don Juan hurried past in his white mantle. "Now play it," said Florestan. Eusebius consented; and in the recess of a window we listened. Eusebius played as though he was inspired, and led forward countless forms, filled with the liveliest, warmest life; it seemed that the inspiration of the moment gave to his fingers a power beyond the ordinary measure of their cunning.

It is true that Florestan's whole applause was expressed in nothing more than a happy smile, and the remark that the variations might have been written by Beethoven or Franz Schubert, had either of these been a pianoforte virtuoso; but how surprised he was, when, turning to the title-page, he read, *" 'La ci darem la mano,' varié pour le pianoforte par Frédéric Chopin, Oeuvre 2,"* and with what astonishment we both cried out "An Opus 2!" How our faces glowed, as we wondered, exclaiming: "That is something reasonable once more—Chopin—I never heard of the name—who can he be?—in any case a genius—"

On Chopin

I could not describe the scene. Heated with wine, Chopin, and our own enthusiasm, we went to Master Raro,* who, with a smile, and displaying but little curiosity for Opus 2, said, "Bring me the Chopin! I know you and your new-fangled enthusiasm!" We promised to bring it the next day. Eusebius soon bade us goodnight; I remained a short time with Master Raro; Florestan, who had been for some time without a habitation, hurried through the moonlit streets to my house. At midnight I found him lying on the sofa with his eyes closed. "Chopin's variations," he began as if in a dream, "are constantly running through my head; the whole is dramatic and Chopin-like; the introduction is so self-concentrated—do you remember Leporello's springs, in thirds?—that seems to me somewhat unfitted to the whole: but the thema—why did he write it in B flat?— The variations, the finale, the adagio, these are indeed something; genius burns through every measure. Naturally, dear Julius, Don Juan, Zerlina, Leporello, and Masetto are the *dramatis personae;* Zerlina's answer in the thema has a sufficiently enamoured character; the first variation expresses a kind of coquettish courteousness,—and the Spanish grandee flirts most amiably with the peasant girl in it.

"This leads of itself into the second, which is at once comic, confidential, disputatious, as though two lovers were chasing each other, and laughing more than usual about it. How all this is changed in the third!

* Wieck, whose daughter became Schumann's wife.

115

It is filled with moonshine and fairy magic; Masetto keeps at a distance, swearing audibly, without making any effect on Don Juan. And now the fourth, what do you think of that? Eusebius played it altogether correctly—how boldly, how wantonly it springs forward to meet the man, though the adagio (it seems quite natural to me that Chopin repeats the first part) is in B-flat minor, as it should be, for in its commencement it presents a moral warning to Don Juan.

It is at once mischievous and beautiful that Leporello listens behind the hedge, laughing and jesting, that oboes and clarinets enchantingly allure, and that the B-flat major, in full bloom, correctly designates the first kiss of love.

"But all this is nothing compared to the last";—have you any more wine, Julius?—"that is the whole of Mozart's finale, popping champagne corks, ringing glasses! Leporello's voice between, the grasping, torturing demons, the fleeing Don Juan—and then the end, that beautifully soothes, and closes all." Florestan concluded by saying that he had never experienced feelings similar to those awakened by this finale, except in Switzerland. When the evening sunlight of a beautiful day gradually creeps up towards the highest peaks, and when the last beam vanishes, there comes a moment when we think we see the white Alpine giants close their eyes. We feel that we have beheld a heavenly apparition."

"And now awake to new dreams, Julius, and sleep!" —"Dear Florestan," I answered, "these confidential

On Chopin

feelings are perhaps praiseworthy, although somewhat
subjective; but as deeply as yourself I bend before
Chopin's spontaneous genius, his lofty aims, his mastership!"—and after that we fell asleep.

By Franz Liszt

In analyzing the works of Chopin we meet with beauties of a high order, expressions which are quite new, and a harmonic tissue which is as original as it is erudite.* In his compositions boldness is always justified; his richness, or even exuberance, is never allowed to interfere with clearness; singularity is never permitted to degenerate into an uncouth fantasticality; his sculpturing never wants order; the luxury of his ornamentation is never allowed to overload the chaste eloquence of his leading outlines. His finest works abound in combinations which may be described as forming an epoch in the handling of musical style. They are daring, brilliant, always attractive; but they disguise their profundity by so much grace, that it is a work of difficulty to free ourselves from their magical enthralment sufficiently to form in cold blood a judgment of their

* The extensive volume on Chopin of which this is an excerpt was first published in 1852.

theoretical value. Their worth, however, has already been admitted; but it will be estimated more highly when the time arrives for a critical examination of the vast services rendered by them to art during that period of its course which Chopin traversed.

It is to Chopin that we owe extended chords played together in arpeggio or *en batterie;* those chromatic sinuosities such striking samples of which are seen in his pages, those little groups of super-added notes which drop like delicate drops of pearly dew upon the melodic figure. Hitherto this species of adornment had only been modelled on the *fioriture* of the grand old school of Italian song; embellishments for the voice, although they had become stereotyped and had grown monotonous, had been servilely copied by the pianoforte; Chopin endowed them with a charm of novelty, surprise and variety, quite unsuitable for the singer but in perfect keeping with the character of the instrument. It was he who invented those admirable harmonic progressions which have imparted a serious character to pages which, by reason of the lightness of their subjects, made no pretensions to importance.

But what matters about the subjects? Is it not rather the idea which the subject develops, the emotion with which it vibrates, and which expands it, elevates it, ennobles it? Although the subjects of La Fontaine's masterpieces, and the titles so modest, how tender is their melancholy, and what subtlety and sagacity do they reveal! Just as unassuming are the titles and the subjects of Chopin's "Studies" and "Preludes," and yet the compositions which are thus modestly named are none the less types of perfection in a mode which he himself created, and stamped, as he did all his other works, with the deep impress of his poetic genius. Written when his career was only just beginning, they are marked by a youthful vigor not found in some of his later works, even when they are more elaborate and finished, and richer in combinations—a vigor which we altogether miss in the subsequent works, which are marked by over-excited sensibility and morbid irritability, and which give painful indications of his own condition of suffering and exhaustion.

It is not our intention to discuss the development of pianoforte music in the language of the schools; we might dissect his magnificent pages, which furnish so fine a field for scientific observation. We should in the first instance analyze his nocturnes, ballads, impromptus, scherzos, so full of refinements of harmony never before heard, bold and startling in their originality; and we should also examine his polonaises, mazurkas, waltzes and boleros. But this is not the time or place for such an examination, which would only be of interest to adepts in counterpoint and thoroughbass.

His works have become known and popular because of the *feeling* which they contain—feeling of a kind pre-eminently romantic, individual, subjective; peculiar to the composer and yet evoking immediate response and sympathy; appealing not merely to the heart of his country, indebted to him for yet another glory, but to all who are capable of being touched by the misfortunes

On Chopin

of exile or affected by the tenderness of human love.

Not content with his success in that field in which he was free to fill up with such perfect grace the outlines he had himself selected, Chopin also wished to imprison his thoughts and ideas by classical fetters. His concertos and sonatas are, indeed, beautiful, but they reveal much more effort than inspiration. His creative genius was imperious, fantastic, impulsive, and the beauties of his work were only fully manifested in absolute freedom. We cannot help thinking that he did violence to the peculiar nature of his genius when he endeavored to subject it to rules, to classifications and to regulations not of his own making, and which he could not bend into harmony with the requirements of his own mind. He was one of those original souls whose graces are only fully revealed when they have cut themselves adrift from all bondage and float on at their own wild will, controlled only by the ever-changing impulses of their own mobile natures.

Chopin was probably led to desire this double success by the example of his friend Mickiewicz, who, having been the first to bestow romantic poetry upon his native land, forming as early as the year 1818, by the publication of his "Dziady" and his romantic ballads, a school of his own Sclavic literature, afterwards showed by publishing his "Graznza" and "Wallenrod" that he could triumph over the difficulties opposed to inspiration by classic restrictions, and that, when holding the classic lyre of the ancient poets, he was still a master. We do not think Chopin's success, in his analogous attempts, was equal to that of Mickiewicz; within the outline of an angular and rigid mold he could not retain that floating and indeterminate contour which so charms us in his graceful conceptions. He could not bend and force to fit those unyielding lines, that shadowy and sketchy indecision, which disguises the skeleton and the whole framework of form and yet drapes it in the mists of floating vapors such as surround the white-bosomed maids of Ossian when, from their abode in the changing, drifting, blinding clouds, they permit mortals to catch sight of a vague yet lovely outline.

And yet some of Chopin's efforts in the classic sphere are resplendent with rare dignity of style, and among them may be found passages of wondrous interest and of astonishing grandeur. As an example we may cite the Adagio of the Second Concerto,* which he was fond of playing frequently, and for which he always showed a decided preference. The principal phrase is of admirable breadth, and the accessory details are in his best style. It alternates with a recitative in a minor key, which seems to be its antistrophe. The whole movement is of an almost ideal perfection; its expression is now radiant with light and anon full of tender pathos. It is as if one had selected a happy vale of Tempé, a brilliant landscape flooded with the glow and luster of summer, as the background for the rehearsal of some appalling scene of mortal anguish, even amidst the incomparable magnificence of external nature a bitter and irreparable regret seizes on the fiercely throb-

* In F minor.

bing heart. This contrast is heightened by a fusion of
tones and a softening down of somber hues which prevent the intrusion of anything rude or brusque which
might awaken dissonance in the touching impression
produced, which saddens joy and at the same time
soothes and softens the bitterness of sorrow.

We cannot pass in silence the Funeral March in the
First Sonata which was arranged for the orchestra, and
performed for the first time at his own funeral. Could
any other accents have been found which would have
expressed with like heartbreaking effect the emotions
and the tears which should accompany to his last long
sleep one who had so sublimely taught how great losses
should be mourned? We once heard a native of his own
land say, "These pages could only have been written by
a Pole!" Everything that the funeral train of a whole
nation lamenting its own ruin and death can be conceived to feel of desolating woe and majestic grief
wails in the musical ring of this passing bell, mourns
in the toll of this solemn knell, as it escorts the mighty
cortege on its journey to the silent city of the dead.

The intensity of mysterious hope; the pious appeal
to superhuman pity, to infinite mercy, to the stern justice which numbers every cradle and watches every
tomb; the lofty resignation which has wreathed halos
so luminous around so much grief; the grand endurance
of so many and so great disasters with the inspired
heroism of Christian martyrs who knew not despair—
all resound in this melancholy chant which breaks the
heart by its suppliant voice. All that is purest, all that is

holiest, all that is most trustful and most hopeful in the hearts of children, women and priests, quivers and trembles in that piece with vibrations which are irresistible. We feel that it is not merely that we mourn the death of one single warrior who leaves other warriors to avenge him, rather has a whole race of warriors forever fallen, leaving only wailing women, weeping children and helpless priests to chant their mournful dirge.

And yet this Mélopée, so funereal and so charged with devastating woe, is full of such penetrating sweetness that we can scarcely believe it had its origin upon earth. These sounds, which seem to chill by awe and soften by distance the wild passion of human anguish, induce most profound meditation, as if they were sung by angels and came floating from the heavens—the cry of a nation's anguish appealing at the very throne of the Eternal! It is a wail of human grief attuned by the lyres of countless seraphs! The sublime sorrow of the plaint is never for a moment troubled by either cries, or hoarse groans, or impious blasphemies, or furious imprecations, but falls on the ear gently as the rhythmed sighs of angels.

The antique face of grief is altogether shut out; no sound recalls Cassandra's fury, Priam's prostration, Hecuba's fury, or the despair of the Trojan captives. A sublime faith destroys in the survivors of this Christian Ilium the bitterness of anguish and the cowardice of despair, and their sorrow is no longer tinged with any weakness. Lifting itself up from the soil wet with tears and blood, it springs upwards to call upon God; having no more to hope from earth, it supplicates the Supreme Judge of heaven with prayers so poignant that in listening our very hearts break under the weight of a divine compassion.

If we imagine that all Chopin's compositions are lacking in the feelings which he saw fit to suppress in this great work, we shall be mistaken, for this is not the case. Human nature is probably not able to always maintain this mood of energetic abnegation and courageous submission. There are, in many passages of his writings breathings of stifled rage and of suppressed anger, many of his studies and scherzos picture a concentrated exasperation and despair, which are at one time manifested in bitter irony, at another in intolerant pride. These gloomy apostrophes of his muse have not been so well understood or attracted so much attention as his more tenderly colored poems, and the personal character of Chopin no doubt had much to do with this general misconception. Being kind, courteous, affable, and of tranquil and almost joyful manners, he would not allow those secret convulsions which tormented him to be even suspected.

It was not indeed easy to comprehend his character; a thousand subtle shades mingled, crossed, contradicted and disguised each other, and rendered it at first view almost undecipherable. As is customary with the Sclaves, it was difficult to fathom the deep recesses of his mind. With them loyalty, candor, familiarity, or a captivating ease of manner do not by any means imply confidence or impulsive frankness.

Chopin's frail and feeble organization did not permit him any energetic expression of his passions, and his friends saw only the gentle and affectionate side of his nature.

Almost stifling under the expression of feelings violently kept down, using his art only to repeat and rehearse for himself his own internal tragedy, he first wearied emotion and then began to subtilize it. His melodies are actually tormented; a sensibility which was nervous and restless led him to an obstinate persistence in handling and re-handling them, and to a continuous pursuit of the tortured *motifs*, which produce upon us an impression as painful as the sight of those mental or physical agonies which we know can only be relieved by death itself. Chopin was the victim of a hopeless disease which each year became more envenomed, took him, while he was still young, from those who loved him, and at length laid him in his silent grave. And as in the fair form of some beautiful victim, we may trace the marks of the grasping claws of the fierce bird which has destroyed it, so in the compositions of which we have been speaking we may find the traces of those bitter sufferings by which his heart was devoured.

* * *

The energetic rhythm of Chopin's polonaises galvanizes into life all the torpor of our indifference. In them are embodied the noblest traditional feelings of the Poland of a bygone age, through them breathe the stern resolve and the reflective gravity of the Poles of other days. Usually of a warlike character, bravery and valor are in these polonaises rendered with a simplicity of expression which was a distinctive characteristic of this warlike people. They bring before the imagination with vivid intensity the ancient Poles as they are described in their chronicles, endowed with a powerful organization, a refined intelligence, unconquerable courage, a piety profound and in every way touching, with all which qualities were combined an innate courtesy and gallantry which never forsook them, whether on the eve of a battle, in the very midst of its exciting scenes, in the flush of victory or in the gloomy pallor of defeat.

So much a part of their nature was this chivalric gallantry and courtesy that notwithstanding the restraints which it was their habit to impose upon their women— restraints not unlike those of their neighbors and foes, the infidels of Stamboul, keeping them within the limits of home life and ever reserving legal wardships over them, that those characteristic qualities yet show themselves in their annals, wherein they have known how to glorify and immortalize queens who were saints, peasants who became queens, lovely subjects for whom some imperilled and others even lost crowns—a terrible Sforza and an intriguing d'Arquien, a coquettish Gurzaga.

* * *

127

As we listen to some of the polonaises of Chopin, we can almost hear the firm, nay, the heavy and resolute tread of men, who were with the noble pride of unblenching courage standing up to face all the bitter injustice which could be put upon them by a most cruel and restless destiny. We can almost see passing before us such magnificent groups as those painted by Paolo Veronese—groups arrayed in the rich costumes of times long gone by: gold brocades, velvets, damasked satins, sables silvery, soft and flexible, hanging sleeves thrown gracefully back on the shoulders, sabers beautifully embossed, boots red like trampled blood or burnished gold, sashes with broad fringes, close chemisettes, rustling trains, stomachers strewn with pearls, head-gear ornamented with rubies or glittering with emeralds, light slippers richly adorned with amber, gloves perfumed with the luxurious attar of the harems.

These and similar vivid groups stand out from the background of days long gone by; gorgeous Persian carpets are under their feet, filagreed furniture of Constantinople stands around them, and everything is impressed with the measureless prodigality of the great magnates who quaffed wines from the fountains of Tokay out of ruby goblets richly embossed with medallions, who caused their fleet steeds of Araby to be shod with silver, who topped their escutcheons with the crown which the turn of an election might turn into a royal one—the crown which caused them to despise other titles, and was won as a token of their glorious equality.

People who saw the polonaise danced even as recently as the early years of the nineteenth century protested that its style was so much changed that it was even almost impossible to divine its original character. Just as the very few national dances have been able to preserve their original purity, so, when we remember the changes which have occurred in Poland, it is not difficult to conclude that the polonaise has greatly degenerated. The polonaise has no rapid movements, nor has it, in the artistic sense, any of those true "steps" which are meant for display rather than for the exhibition of a seductive grace.

We can easily understand that when those who dance it are deprived of all those accessories which are requisite to enable them to give life to its simple form by dignified yet vivid gestures, and by appropriate and expressive pantomime, the polonaise must of necessity lose all its haughty import and all its pompous self-sufficiency. It has thus become altogether monotonous, a mere ambling promenade, and awakens but little interest. We cannot see it danced under the old régime by men and women clad in the ancient costumes, nor can we listen while they describe it; and we can therefore form no notion of the numerous incidents and the scenic pantomime which once made it so effective. This dance is one of those rare exceptions designed to show off, not the women but the men, to exhibit manly beauty, to set off noble and dignified deportment and martial yet courtly bearing.

And do not these two epithets, "martial yet courtly," wellnigh define the Polish character? The very name of the dance is, in the Polish tongue, of the masculine gender, and it is only through a complete misconception of the purpose and character of the dance that its name has in some other languages been transformed into a feminine noun.

* * *

By his peculiar style of playing, Chopin imparted with the most fascinating effect this constant rocking, making the melody undulate to and fro like a skiff driven over the bosom of tossing waves. This manner of execution, which set so peculiar a seal upon his own style of performance, was first indicated by the words *tempo rubato* affixed to his works; a *tempo* broken, agitated, interrupted; a movement flexible while it was abrupt and languishing, and as vacillating as the flame under the fluctuating breath which agitates it. This direction is no longer found in his later productions; he was persuaded that if the player understood them he would divine this regular irregularity. All his compositions ought to be played with this accentuated and measured swaying and rocking, though it is difficult for those who never heard him play to catch hold of this secret of their proper execution. He was desirous to impart this style to his many pupils, especially those of his own land. His countrymen, or rather his countrywomen, seized upon it with that facility with which they comprehend everything relating to poetry or the emotions—an innate, intuitive grasping of his meaning aided them in following all the fluctuations of his depths of ethereal and spiritual azure.

* * *

He only sought in the great classic models and *chefs-d'oeuvre* that which was in harmony with his own soul; he was pleased by all that stood in relation to that, while that which did not resemble it scarcely received justice from him; uniting as he did in himself those qualities of passion and grace which are so often incompatible, he possessed great accuracy of judgment and was preserved from petty partiality, but he was only slightly attracted by the greatest beauties or the highest merits if they happened to wound any phase of his own poetic conceptions. In spite of the high admiration he felt for Beethoven's works, certain parts of them always appeared to him to be too rudely sculptured; their structure was too robust to please him, their wrath was too tempestuous and their passion too overwhelming, the lion-marrow which fills Beethoven's every phase was matter too substantial for the taste of Chopin, and to him the Raphaelic and seraphic profiles wrought into the nervous and powerful creations of that great genius were almost painful from the cutting force of the contrast in which they are so often set.

Notwithstanding the charm which he admittedly found in some of Schubert's melodies, Chopin would not willingly listen to those in which the contours were too rugged for his refined ear, those where the suffering lies exposed, where we can almost feel the flesh palpitate and hear the bones crash and crack beneath the rude grasp of sorrow.

* * *

About Schubert he once said that "the sublime is desecrated when it is succeeded by the trivial or the commonplace." Among composers for the piano Hummel was one of those whom he read and re-read with most pleasure. In Chopin's eyes Mozart was the ideal type, the poet *par excellence,* because he condescended more rarely than any other composer to go down the inclined plane leading from what is beautiful to what is commonplace. Mozart's father was once present at a performance of "Idomeneo," and afterwards thus reproached his son: "You are wrong in putting in it nothing for the long-eared ones"; but it was precisely for such omissions that he was admired by Chopin.

On Schubert

By Robert Schumann

The musician who visits Vienna for the first time, awhile delights in the festive life of the streets, and often stands admiringly before the door of St. Stephen's Tower; but he soon remembers how near to the city lies a cemetery, containing something more worthy—for him—of regard than all the city boasts, —the spot where two of the glorious ones of his art rest, only a few steps apart.

No doubt, then, many a young musician has wandered like me (1838) to the Währinger Cemetery, after the first few days of excitement in Vienna, to lay his flowery gift on those graves, even were it but a wild rosebush, such as I found planted on Beethoven's grave. Franz Schubert's resting place was undecorated. One warm desire of my life was fulfilled; I gazed long on those sacred graves, almost envying the one buried between them—a certain Earl O'Donnell, if I am not mistaken.*

* According to other sources, the grave that occupied the exalted position between Beethoven and Schubert was that

133

Schumann

The first time of gazing on a great man, of pressing his hand, is for every one an earnestly-desired moment. It had never been possible for me to meet either of the two whom I venerate most highly among all modern artists; but after this visit to their graves, I wished I could have stood by the side of a man who loved either one of them most dearly—if possible, his own brother. On the way home, I remembered that Schubert's brother Ferdinand, to whom he had been much attached, was still living. I sought him out, and found that he bore a strong resemblance to the bust that stands beside Schubert's grave; shorter than Franz, but strongly built, with a face expressive of honesty as well as of musical ability. He knew me from that veneration for his brother which I have so often publicly professed; * told me and showed me many things, of which, with his permission, I have already spoken in our paper, under the heading "Reliques." Finally, he allowed me to see those treasures of Schubert's composition, which he still possesses. The sight of this hoard of riches thrilled me with joy; where to begin, where to leave

---

of one Hardmuth. However, the Währinger cemetery has in modern times been converted to a park named in honor of Schubert, following the removal of the remains of the two composers (in 1888) to "graves of honor" in the vast Central Cemetery.—Ed.

* Nearly ten years before (in 1829) in a letter from Heidelberg to Friedrich Wieck, Schumann wrote rapturously of "my only Schubert," and continued with a comparison to Jean Paul Richter which we find him making again later in this article.—Ed.

off! Among other things, he directed my attention to the scores of several symphonies, many of which have never yet been heard, but are laid on the shelf and prejudged as too heavy and turgid.

One must understand Vienna, its peculiar circumstances with regard to concerts, and the difficulties attendant on bringing together the necessary material for great performances, before one can forgive the city where Schubert lived and labored, that only his songs, but his grand instrumental works seldom or never, are brought before the public. Who knows how long the symphony of which we speak today, might not have lain buried in dust and darkness, had I not at once arranged with Ferdinand Schubert, to send it immediately to the direction of the Gewandhaus concerts in Leipzig, or rather, to the directing artist himself, whose fine glance perceives even the most timid of new budding beauties,—and necessarily, therefore, the dazzling splendors of masterly perfection. My hopes were fulfilled. The symphony went to Leipzig, was listened to, understood, again heard, and received with joyous and almost universal admiration. The busy publishing house of Breitkopf and Haertel purchased the work, and now it lies before me in separate parts; for the benefit of the world, I hope it will soon appear in score also.*

* It was not until twenty-seven years later that the work by which Schubert is best known to the world—the "Unfinished" symphony—had its first performance. During all this time it remained in the possession of Anselm Hüttenbrenner,

I must say at once, that he who is not yet acquainted with this symphony, knows very little about Schubert; and this, when we consider all that he has given to art outside of this work, will appear to many as too exaggerated praise. Partly, no doubt, because composers have been so often advised, to their own injury, that it is better for them—after Beethoven—to abstain from symphonic plans; which advice, notwithstanding, with the state of feeling that has given rise to it, we can scarcely consider as unreasonable. For we have lately had few orchestral works of consequence; and those few have interested us rather as illustrations of their composer's progress, than that of art or as creations of decided influence with the masses.

Many have been absolute reflections of Beethoven; and it is scarcely necessary to mention those tiresome manufacturers of symphonies, with power enough to shadow forth the powder and perruques of Mozart and Haydn, but not indeed the heads that wore them. Berlioz is thoroughly French, and we are too much accustomed to regard him merely as an interesting foreigner and rattle pate.

The hope I had always entertained—and many no doubt, with me—that Schubert, who had shown himself through many other kinds of composition, so firm in form, so rich in imaginativeness, so many sided, would also treat the symphony and find that mode of

a lifelong friend of the composer, who finally relinquished it for performance by the *Gesellschaft der Musikfreunde* of Vienna in 1865.—Ed.

treatment certain to impress the public, is here realized in the noblest manner. Assuredly he never proposed to excel Beethoven's Ninth Symphony but, an
industrious artist, he continually drew forth his creations from his own resources, one symphony after
another.

The only thing that seems to us objectionable in the
publication of this seventh symphony, or that may lead
even to a misunderstanding of the work, is the fact
that the world now receives it without having followed
its creator's development of this form through its fore-
runners. Perhaps, however, the bolts may now be
drawn from the others; the least of them must possess
Schubertian significance. Viennese symphony writers
did not need to wander very far in search of the laurel
they are so much in need of, for in a suburb of Vienna,
in Ferdinand Schubert's study, they might have found
sevenfold richer booty, leaf heaped on leaf. And here,
too, was the place of all others which they should have
crowned with the laurel! But it often happens in the
world that such opportunities are neglected! Should the
conversation turn upon——, the Viennese never know
how to finish with their praise of their own Franz
Schubert; when they are among themselves, it does not
seem as if they thought much of one or the other.

But let us leave these things, and refresh ourselves
with the wealth of mind that in its fulness overflows
this glorious work! Vienna, with its tower of St. Stephen, its lovely women, its public pageantry, its Danube that garlands it with countless watery ribbons; this

Vienna spreading over the blooming plain, and reaching toward the higher mountains; Vienna, with its
reminiscences of the great German masters, must be a
fertile domain for the musician's fancy to revel in.
Often when gazing on the city from the heights above,
I have thought how frequently Beethoven's eyes may
have glanced restlessly over the distant line of the
Alps; how Mozart may have dreamily followed the
course of the Danube, as it seems to vanish amid bush
and wood; and how Haydn may have looked up to
the tower shaking his head at its dizzy height. If we
draw together the tower, the Danube, and the distant
Alps, casting over the whole a soft Catholic incense
vapour, we shall have a fair picture of Vienna; and
when the charming, living landscape stands before us,
chords will vibrate that never resounded within us
before.

On leaving Schubert's symphony, the bright, blooming romantic life of Vienna appears to me clearer than
ever; such works ought to be born amid precisely
such surroundings. But I shall not attempt to set the
symphony in its fitting soil; different ages select different bases for their texts and pictures; where the
youth of eighteen hears a world famous occurrence in
a musical work, a man only perceives some rustic
event, while the musician probably never thought of
either, but simply gave the best music that he happened to feel within him just then.

But every one must acknowledge that the outer
world, sparkling today, gloomy tomorrow, often

deeply impresses the inward feeling of the poet or the musician; and all must recognise, while listening to this symphony, that it reveals to us something more than mere fine melody, mere ordinary joy and sorrow, such as music has already expressed in a hundred ways —that it leads us into a region which we never before explored, and consequently can have no recollection of. Here we find, besides the most masterly technicalities of musical composition, life in every vein, coloring down to the finest grade of possibility, sharp expression in detail, meaning throughout, while over the whole is thrown that glow of romanticism that everywhere accompanies Franz Schubert. And then the heavenly length * of the symphony, like that of one of Jean Paul's romances in four thick volumes, never able to come to an end, for the very best reason—in order to leave the reader able to go on romancing for himself. How refreshing is this feeling of overflowing wealth! With others we always tremble for the conclusion, troubled lest we find ourselves disappointed.

It would be incomprehensible whence Schubert had all at once acquired this sparkling, sportive mastery of the orchestra, did we not know that this symphony had

* This famous phrase first occurs in a letter written by Schumann to Clara Wieck (soon to be his wife) on the day of the first rehearsal in Leipzig of the C major symphony (Dec. 11, 1839). "All the instruments are like human voices" he writes, "and it is all so intellectual; and then the instrumentation, in spite of Beethoven! And the length of it—such a heavenly length, like a four volume novel; why, it is longer than the Ninth Symphony."—Ed.

been preceded by six others, and that it was written in the ripest years of manly power (on the score is the date, "March, 1828"; Schubert died in November). We must grant that he possessed an extraordinary talent, in attaining to such peculiar treatment of separate instruments, such mastery of orchestral masses—they often seem to converse like human voices and choruses —although he scarcely heard any of his own instrumental works performed during his life. Save in some of Beethoven's works, I have not observed so striking and deceptive a resemblance to the voice, in the treatment of instruments; Meyerbeer, in his treatment of the human voice, attains precisely the opposite effect. Another proof of the genuine, manly inspiration of this symphony, is its complete independence of the Beethoven symphonies. And how correct, how prudent in judgment, Schubert's genius displays itself here! As if conscious of his more modest power, he avoids imitating the grotesque forms, the bold proportions that meet us in Beethoven's later works; he gives us a creation of the most graceful form possible, which, in spite of its novel intricacies never strays from the happy medium, but always returns again to the central point.

Every one who closely studies this symphony, must agree with me. At first, every one will feel a little embarrassed by the brilliancy and novelty of the instrumentation, the length and breadth of form, the charming variety of vital feeling, the entirely new world that opens to us—just as the first glance at any thing to which we are unaccustomed, embarrasses us; but a delightful feeling remains, as though we had been listening to a lovely tale of enchantment, we feel that the composer was master of his subject, and after a time, its intricacies and connections all become clear to us. The feeling of certainty is produced at once by the splendid, romantic introduction, over which, notwithstanding, a mysterious veil seems to have been drawn here and there. The passage from this into the allegro is wholly new; the tempo does not seem to change, yet we reach the port, we know not how. It would not give us or others any pleasure to analyse the separate movements; for to give an idea of the novel-like character that pervades the whole symphony, the entire work ought to be transcribed.

Yet I cannot take leave of the second movement—which speaks to us with such touching voices—without a few words. There is a passage in it, where a horn calls from a distance, that seems to have descended from another sphere. And every other instrument seems to listen, as if aware that a heavenly guest had glided into the orchestra.

The symphony produced such an effect among us as none has produced since Beethoven's. Artists and connoisseurs united in its praise, and I heard a few words spoken by the master who had studied it with the utmost care for its perfect success, that I should have been only too happy, had such a thing been possible to report to the living Schubert, as the gladdest of glad tidings. Years must pass, perhaps, before the

work will be thoroughly made at home in Germany;
but there is no danger that it will ever be overlooked
or forgotten; it bears within it the core of everlasting
youth.

And thus my visit to those honored graves, reminding me of a relation of one of the great departed,
became doubly a reward to me. I received my first
recompense on the day itself; for I found, on Beethoven's grave, a steel pen which I have treasured up
carefully ever since. I never use it save on festal occa-
sians, as to-day; I trust that good things may have
proceeded from it!

On Weber

By Richard Wagner

In the midst of the Bohemian forests, as old as the
world, lies the Wolfsschlucht,—the wolf's ravine,—
the legend of which lived among the people up to
the time of the Thirty Years' War, which put an end
to the last traces of German glory.* Then, however,
like so many mystic memories, it died away. Even at
that time the majority only knew of the mysterious
ravine through hearsay; it was said that this or that
hunter, wandering sometime through wild and track-
less forest solitudes, on unknown trails and in directions which he could not define, had suddenly chanced,
he knew not how, upon the edge of the Wolfsschlucht.
Such a hunter would tell of the horrible things that
he had seen on gazing down into it—things that made
his hearer cross himself and commend himself to his
patron saint with the prayer that he might never be
lost in that region. Even while approaching the hunter

* From Wagner's "Art Life and Theories."

had heard a singular sound; stifled sobs and groans swept through the broad branches of the old fir-trees, which of themselves moved their dark tops hither and thither; and all this while the wind was perfectly still. Reaching the edge, he peered down into an abyss, into whose depths his eye could not penetrate. Rocky fragments raised themselves in the shape of human limbs and ghastly, distorted faces; beside them heaps of black stones took the forms of frogs and lizards; farther down in the depths these forms appeared to be alive; they moved, crawled, and rolled away in clumsy, chaotic masses; the ground beneath them could not be distinguished. Only pale mists rose constantly up from it, and spread abroad pestilential odors; here and there they separated and stretched themselves out into great sheets that took on the forms of human beings with convulsively distorted features. In the midst of all this horror there sat upon a rotten stump an enormous owl, stupid with the torpor of the daytime; and opposite to this was a dark cavern in the rocks, the entrance to which was watched by two monsters horribly formed of serpents, toads, and lizards. These, apparently endowed with life, like all that the abyss concealed, lay in a sleep like death; and whatever moved seemed only the movement of one who dreamed; so that the frightful thought occurred to the hunter—how all this brood would come to life when midnight came!

But what he heard filled him with more horror than what he saw. A stormy wind, that moved nothing, and the breath of which he could not feel, howled across the chasm—then ceased suddenly, as though listening to itself, only to break forth again with more furious rage than ever. Frightful shrieks rose from below; and then a flock of countless birds of prey flew about the depths of the abyss, raised itself like a black covering above the ravine, and sank back again into the darkness. Their croakings sounded to the hunter like the groans of the damned, and pierced his heart with an anguish never felt before. He had never heard such a shriek—beside which all the croaking of the ravens seemed to him like the songs of nightingales,—and now again all was silent. Every motion startled him; there only seemed to be a heavy crawling in the abyss below, and the owl flapped his wings once heavily, as though in a dream.

The most fearless hunter—the one best acquainted with the midnight terrors of the woods,—fled away aghast, like a timid deer; and without minding the path, rushed directly for the nearest loiterer—the nearest hut—only to meet a human being to whom he could narrate the horrors he had seen—which, nevertheless, he never could find language to describe. How could he rid himself of such a recollection?

Happy is the youth who bears in his heart a pure, true love! That alone can drive away any terrors that he can imagine befalling him. Is not his beloved his sheltering spirit, his guardian angel, that follows him everywhere, shines within him, and diffuses peace and warmth throughout his inner life? Since he has loved,

145

he is no longer the rough, harsh hunter, revelling in blood and the slaughter of game. His beloved has taught him to see the diviner part of the creation, and to hear the voices that speak to him from the mysterious silence of the woods. He feels himself seized with pity now, when the deer springs through the underbrush; he fulfils the duties of his calling with reluctant trembling, and could weep when he sees the tears in the eyes of the noble prey lying at his feet.

And yet he cannot but love the rough labor of the woods; for he has to thank his skill as a hunter and his prowess as a marksman, for the privilege of striving for the hand of his sweetheart. The forester's daughter must only belong to her father's successor in the office; and to gain this inheritance of forestry he must succeed in the trial of marksmanship on the day of his marriage; if he does not show then that he is a thoroughly sure shot, he fails of his reward—he loses both forestership and bride! His heart must be firm and strong, his sight unwavering; his hand must not tremble.

But the nearer the decisive moment approaches, the more his good fortune seems to abandon him. Heretofore the most skilful marksman, it often happens to him now to rove all day through the woods without bringing home the most trifling booty. What ill luck pursues him? If it be sympathy with the game that has grown so confiding, why should he miss when he aims at some bird of prey, for whom he has *no* sympathy? Why should he miss even in shooting at a mark, when

146

his object is to carry home to his sweetheart some ribbon he has won, to drive away her anxiety? The old forester shakes his head; his betrothed grows more anxious with every day; our hunter wanders through the woods a prey to gloomy thoughts. He ponders on his ill-luck, and seeks to find a reason for it.

Then there rises in his memory the day when his fate led him to the edge of the Wolfsschlucht; the groaning and sobbing in the pine-branches, the horrible croaking of the flock of night-birds, again confuse his brain. He believes himself a prey to some hellish power, that, jealous of his happiness, has sworn his ruin. And all that he has heard of the Wild Huntsman and his hunt comes back into his memory. This was a hellish confusion of huntsmen, horses, hounds, and stags, that swept by above the forest in the unholy hours of midnight. Woe to him who was in its path! The human heart was too weak to withstand the effect of this chaos of clanging weapons, horrible hunting-calls, horn-blasts, barking of dogs and neighing of horses;—he who had seen the wild hunt was almost sure to die soon after.

The young hunter remembered having heard of the leader of this wild tumult; a godless hunter-prince among the damned, who now as the evil spirit Samiel arose to take his part among his faithful hunters in these nightly forays. It is true, his companion laughs at him, when our hunter is with him, calling this legend of the Wild Huntsman a mere old wives' tale; yet it is this very wild and audacious comrade

that inspires him with the greatest horror. In truth,
he is already a recruit of Samiel; he knows of secret
means—of magic spells—through which one can be
certain of his shot. He tells him that if one appears
at a certain hour at an appointed place, one may banish
evil spirits by the aid of a few trifling vows, and make
them obedient to one's self; if he will but follow him,
he promises to make him bullets that shall hit the
most distant mark according to his wishes;—these are
called "Freikugeln," and he who uses them is a "Freischütz."

The youth listens in amazement. Shall he not believe in invisible spirits, when he remembers how he
—once the best marksman of them all—can no longer
trust his gun that has hitherto never missed its mark?
His peace of mind is gone; faith and hope waver
within him. The decisive day approaches; his fate—
once in his own hands—now seems controlled by hostile powers; he must conquer these with their own
weapons. He has decided. Where shall he appear to
cast the magic bullets? In the Wolfsschlucht. In the
Wolfsschlucht, and at midnight? His hair stands on
end—for now he understands it all. But he understands also that there is no longer any retreat. Hell has
gained him, even if he does not win his bride to-morrow. Shall he give her up? Impossible. Only his courage can save him—and he is brave. And so he
consents.

Once more, late in the evening, he visits the forester's house; pale and with gloomy look, he approaches

On Weber

his beloved. The sight of the sweet, pure girl no
longer soothes him; her faith in God oppresses him
like mockery; who is it that helps *him* to win his
bride?

The leaves rustle gently around the lonely house;
the girl's companion seeks to cheer the saddened pair;
but he sits brooding and staring out into the night.
His sweetheart throws her arms around him; but her
gentle whispers are drowned in the harsh creakings of
the dark fir trees—*that* he hears ever and anon, recalling him to himself as though with the voice of
the deadly terror that is in his heart. Suddenly he tears
himself from the arms of the terrified and anxious
bride:—to possess her he is ready to risk the salvation
of his soul.

He rushes out and away. With wonderful accuracy
he follows the unknown path. The way seems to clear
before him, that leads him to the abyss of horror
where his companion has already made his preparations for the gloomy work. In vain the spirit of his
mother appears, warning him away. The memory of
the maiden that he must lose if he hesitates, urges
him onward. He descends into the ravine and enters
the circle of the hellish conjuror. And hell responds
to him; that which the hunter foresaw as he approached the chasm by day, is now fulfilled at midnight. All around him awakes from its death-like
sleep; becomes alive, turns and stretches itself; the
howling increases to a roar,—the groaning to a rag-
ing bellow; a thousand monsters surround the magic

circle. No shrinking now—or we are lost! Suddenly the Wild Hunt thunders past above his head; his senses reel; he falls unconscious to the ground—and when he wakes again—?

During the night seven magic bullets are cast. Six of them must infallibly hit any mark that may be chosen; but the seventh belongs to him that gave the rest their fortune—and this one will turn as pleases him. The two hunters divide them—the caster of the bullets taking three; the candidate for the maiden's hand takes four.

The prince arrives in person to superintend the arrangements for the trial of the marksman's skill. The hunters waste their bullets in the strife for his favor in the preliminary hunt; it is the seventh bullet which the would-be bridegroom, who now begins again to make constant misses, treasures up for the last decisive shot. For this trial, a white dove that suddenly starts up is pointed out as the mark; he pulls the trigger, and his beloved, who is just approaching with her bridesmaids through the shrubbery, falls wounded, bathed in blood.

Samiel has secured his payment; will he gain the young hunter for his wild hunt—the young hunter whom the darkness of madness has encompassed?

* * *

Such is the legend of the Freischütz. It seems to be the very poem for those Bohemian forests, whose dark and gloomy aspect makes it easily conceivable that the isolated beings that live among them think themselves —if not positively the prey of some demoniac power of nature—at least hopelessly under its control. And in this very characteristic is to be found the specifically German character of this and similar traditions; it is so sharply defined by natural surroundings, that to it alone is to be attributed the origin of that demoniac imagery, which, among other peoples, not equally subject to the influence of nature, rather takes on forms derived from human society, or from ruling religions and metaphysical ideas. Though it may not be wanting in the elements of horror, such imagery is not in the latter case *altogether* horrible; pathos appears through its horror; and regret for the lost paradise of a purely natural life somewhat mitigates the dread of the deserted Mother Nature's vengeance.

What we have described is purely German. Everywhere else we find the devil going about among mankind; forcing witches and enchanters to obey his will and then arbitrarily giving them over to the stake or saving them from death. We even see him appear as a *paterfamilias,* and guard his son with suspicious scrupulousness. But even the roughest peasant no longer believes all this nowadays, for such proceedings are pictured too bluntly as taking place in everyday life— in which he knows they no longer happen; while the secret, mysterious relations of the human heart to the strange nature around it, have not yet come to an end. In its eloquent silence, this latter still speaks to the heart just as it did a thousand years ago; and what was told in the very gray of antiquity is understood today as easily as then. For this reason it is that the legend of *nature* ever remains the inexhaustible resource of the poet in his intercourse with his people.

But only from this very people that invented the legend of the Freischütz, and feels itself today under its influence, could come a musical poet of true genius, who could hit upon the idea of creating a great musical work upon a dramatic basis derived from that legend. If he understood truly the fundamental spirit of the popular poem here presented to him, and felt himself able to call by his music into full and mystic life what was indicated in this characteristic creation,—he knew that he should be fully understood in turn by his people, from the mystic sounds of his overture to the childlike and simple fashioning of the "Jungfern-kranz."

And indeed, in glorifying the old folk-legend of his home, the artist assured himself an unprecedented success. His countrymen both from north and south, from the disciple of Kant's "Kritik der reinen Vernunft" to the readers of the Viennese fashionable journals, united in admiration of the melodies of this pure and deep elegy. The Berlin philosopher stammered out "We twine for thee the maiden's wreath" (Jungfernkranz); the police director repeated enthusiastically "Through the forest, through the meadows"; while the court lackey sang, in hoarse voice, "What is fitting on earth." And I can remember how I studied as a boy, to get the demon-like expression in gesture and voice necessary for the proper harsh perfomance of "Here in this earthly vale of woes." The Austrian grenadiers marched to the Hunter's Chorus; Prince Metternich danced to the music of the Bohemian peasants' "Landler"; and the students of Jena sung the scoffing chorus after their professors. The most opposing tendencies of political life met here in a single point of union; "Der Freischütz" was heard, sung, and danced from one end of Germany to the other.

And you too, promenaders of the Bois de Boulogne, —you too have hummed the melodies of the "Freischütz"; the hand-organs played the Hunter's Chorus in the streets; the *Opéra Comique* did not scorn the "Jungfernkranz"; and the delicious air "How did slumber come upon me?" has repeatedly enchanted the audiences of your salons. But do you understand what you sing? I doubt it greatly. On what my doubt rests, however, it is difficult to say;—not less difficult, certainly, than to explain to you that thoroughly foreign German nature, from which those melodies proceeded. I should almost think myself compelled to begin at the forest—which, by the way, is just what you don't understand. The Bois is something quite different; as different as your "rêverie" is from our "Empfindsamkeit."

We are truly a singular people! "Through the forests, through the meadows," moves us to tears; while we look with dry eyes on thirty-four principalities around us, instead of one united fatherland! You who only go into enthusiasm when "la France" is concerned, must look on this as a decided weakness; but it is precisely this weakness that you must share if you would rightly understand "Through the forests, through the meadows"; for it is this very weakness that you have to thank for the wonderful score of *Der Freischütz,* which you are about to have performed before you with the greatest accuracy—unquestionably for the purpose of learning to understand it in just the way in which it is *impossible* for you to understand it.

You will not forsake Paris and its customs by one hair's-breadth for this purpose; the Freischütz must come *there* and exhibit himself to you; you encourage him to make himself at ease, to do precisely as though he were at home; for you want to hear and see him as he *is,*—no longer in the costume of "Robin des Bois," * but honest and open-hearted—something like the "Postillon de Longjumeau." So you say. But all this is to be done in the "Academie royale de musique," and that worthy establishment has ordinances which must make the feeling of unembarrassed ease decidedly difficult for the poor Freischütz.

It is written there:—Thou shalt dance! But that he does not do; he is far too heavy-spirited for that, and

* A hopelessly butchered version of *Der Freischütz* had been given in Paris under this title several years before. Its charming tunes alone were responsible for a run of nearly three hundred performances. It is Wagner's insinuation in a later essay *(Der Freischütz: A Report to Germany)* that this success, and the hope of duplicating it, was the inspiration for the production at the Opéra.—Ed.

he lets the peasants and maidens do it for him at the tavern. It is written also:—Thou shalt not speak, but shalt sing recitative! But here is a dialogue of the most complete naïveté. It's all very well; but you can't free him from ballet-dancing and singing recitative,—for he is to present himself at the grand opera!

There might be, it is true, a simple method of getting out of the difficulty; and this would be to make an exception for once for the sake of this glorious work. But you will not adopt this means;—for you are only free when you want to be; and in this case, unfortunately, you *don't* want to be. You have heard of the Wolfsschlucht and of a devil, Samiel; and forthwith the machinery of the grand opera comes into your minds; the rest is of no consequence to you. You want ballet and recitative, and you have chosen the most remarkable of your composers to make the music for it. That you have chosen such a one does you honor, and shows that you know how to value our masterpiece. I know no one of the contemporary French musicians who could understand the score of the Freischütz so well as the author of the *Symphonie fantastique,* and would be so capable as he of completing it, if that were necessary. He is a man of genius, and no one recognizes more fully than I the irresistible strength of his poetic force. He has conscientious principles, that permit him to follow the strong bent of his talent, and in every one of his symphonies there is revealed the inner compulsion which the author could not escape. But precisely because of the distin-

guished capabilities of M. Berlioz, I lay before him
with confidence my remarks upon his work.*

The score of *Der Freischütz* is a finished whole, perfectly rounded in every part, as well in thought as in
form. Would not the omission of the smallest part be
to maim or distort the master's work? Have we to
deal here with the re-construction, to suit the needs
of our time, of a score that had its origin in the childhood of art? The re-arrangement of a work which its
author failed to develop sufficiently, through his ignorance of the technical means that are today at our disposal? Every one knows that there is nothing of this
kind to be done; M. Berlioz would repel with indignation a proposition of this character.—No. What is
in question now, is to bring perfect and original work
into concord, with conditions that are exterior to it—
foreign to it. And how shall this be done?

A score sanctified by twenty years of success, in favor
of which the royal academy of music proposes for once
to deviate from the strict rules that exclude foreign
music from its repertoire, in order to take its part in

* In his *A Travers Chants,* Berlioz offers his defense for assisting in this production, asserting that only the fear that
a less qualified musician would be assigned to the task in any
case, led him to write the recitatives and provide for a
ballet. This last need, incidentally, resulted in his orchestration of Weber's *Invitation to the Dance,* which, ironically,
has far outlived the controversy of its first performance.
Berlioz also has a bitter note on the carpentry that was done
with his version after it was established in the repertory
of the Opéra.—Ed.

the most brilliant triumph that any piece ever won in any theatre,—such a score cannot control a few rules of precedent and routine? May it not be demanded that it shall be produced in that primal form that makes up so great a part of its originality?—Yet this is the sacrifice that is asked of us, is it not? Or do you think I am mistaken? Do you think that the ballet and recitative introduced by you would *not* distort the physiognomy of Weber's work? If you replace a simple—often times witty and lively dialogue, by a recitative which always becomes heavy in the mouths of the singers, do you not believe that the characteristic of cordial heartiness will altogether disappear from it—that characteristic that makes the very soul of the Bohemian peasant-scenes? Must not the confidential chat of the two girls in the lovely forest-house necessarily lose its freshness and truth? And however well these recitatives might be arranged, however artistically they might harmonize with the general coloring of the work, they would not the less destroy its symmetry. It is plain that the German composer constantly had regard to the dialogue. The song-pieces embrace but little; and, if utterly overwhelmed by the gigantic recitative that is added, they would lose in sense and consequently in effect.

In this drama, where the *song* has so deep a significance and so important a meaning, you will find none of those noisy combination passages, of those deafening finales, to which the grand opera has accustomed you. In the "Muet de Portici," in the "Huguenots,"

in the "Jewess," it is necessary that the intermediate
passages between the pieces, on account of the considerable dimensions of the latter, should be filled out by
recitative; in this case dialogue would seem petty, ridiculous, and exactly like a parody. How extraordinary it
would be, for instance, if between the grand duet and
the finale of the second act of the "Muet," Masaniello
should suddenly begin to talk; or if, after the combination passages of the fourth act of the "Huguenots,"
Raoul and Valentine should prepare the way for the
grand duet that follows, by a dialogue, even though
it were in the most carefully chosen phraseology! Of
course this would jar upon you; and rightly.

Very good. But what is an aesthetic necessity for
these operas of greater extent, would be, for precisely
the contrary reasons, ruinous for *Der Freischütz,* in
which the song passages embrace so much less.

In regard to this matter, I foresee that where the
scenes conveyed by the dialogue need a dramatic accent, M. Berlioz will give the reins to his fertile fancy;
I can imagine the expression of gloomy energy which
he will give to the scene in which Kaspar tries to weave
his devilish web about his friend, as he presses him to
test the magic bullet, and that he may further win him
over to the standard of hell, asks him the fearful question—"Coward, dost thou believe the sin is not already upon thee? Dost think this eagle has been *given*
to thee?"—I am certain that at this passage deafening
applause will reward the excellent additions of M.
Berlioz; but I am not less certain, that after this recita-

tive Kaspar's energetic, short aria at the close of the act, will pass for a piece of music unworthy of any particular consideration.

Thus you will have something entirely new—something remarkable, if you will; and we, who know *Der Freischütz,* and need no recitative to complete it, shall with pleasure see the works of M. Berlioz enriched by a new creation; but we shall still doubt whether you can be taught by this means to *understand* our Freischütz. You will delight yourselves with varying music, now cheerful, now wild and spirit-like, that will please your ears, yet at the same time affect you with a sense of horror; you will hear songs performed with wonderful perfection, that up to this time have only been sung moderately well for you; a well arranged dramatic declamation will lead you smoothly from one vocal passage to another; and yet you will feel with annoyance the absence of many things to which you are accustomed, and which you can with difficulty do without. The anticipations which will have been nourished with regard to Weber's work, can and must only awaken in you the desire for some new excitement of the senses—just such a desire as the works generally brought before you with such a preparation really fulfil. But your expectations will find themselves disappointed; for this work was created by its author with quite another purpose, and by no means to satisfy the demands of the Royal Academy of Music.

In the passage where, upon our stage, five musicians take up their fiddles and horns at the door of a tavern, and a few sturdy peasant lads whirl their ungraceful sweethearts in the circle of the dance—in this passage *you* will suddenly behold the choreographic celebrities of the day appear before you; you will see that smiling cutter of capers who but yesterday strutted in his fine gold-colored costume, receiving the graceful sylphs one after the other in his arms. The latter will do their best to show you Bohemian peasant dances,—but in vain; you will continually miss their pirouettes and artistic caperings. Yet they will still give you enough of this sort of thing to transport you, in fancy, to the sphere of your customary enjoyments; they will recall to you the brilliant works of your own famous authors, in which you have so often revelled, and you will demand at least a piece like "William Tell" in which also hunters, shepherds, and various other charming things appropriate to country life, appear.

But after these dances you will have nothing more of that kind; in the first act you have nothing but the air "Through the forests, through the meadows," a drinking song of twenty to eighty bars, and, instead of a noisy finale, the singular musical outpourings of a hellish rascal, which you certainly will not receive as an aria.

Yet no!—I am mistaken. You will have whole scenes of recitative of such strong musical originality as (I am convinced) few have had before; for I know how the brilliant invention of your distinguished composer will feel itself stimulated to add nothing but beautiful and strong passages to the masterpiece that he so honors and admires. It is precisely for this reason that you will not learn to understand *Der Freischütz;* and—who knows?—perhaps what you do hear of it will destroy in you the wish to make acquaintance with it in its simple and primitive form.

If it could really appear before you in its purity and simplicity; if, instead of the complicated, intricate dances that on your stage will accompany the modest bridal procession, you could only hear the little song that, as I said, the Berlin philosophical student hums as he goes; if, instead of the exquisite recitative, you could hear the simple dialogue that every German student knows by heart—would you even then gain a *true* comprehension of *Der Freischütz?* Would it excite among you the unanimous applause which the "Muet de Portici" called forth with us? Ah—I doubt it greatly; and perhaps the same doubt passed like a dark cloud over M. Berlioz's spirit when the director of your grand opera commissioned him to provide *Der Freischütz* with ballet and recitative.

It is a great piece of good fortune that it was precisely M. Berlioz, who was entrusted with this task; certainly no German musician would have ventured, out of regard for the work and the master, to undertake such a matter; and in France no one but M. Berlioz is capable of such an attempt. At least we have the certainty that everything down to the seemingly least important note, will be respected; that nothing will be struck out, and only exactly so much added as is necessary to satisfy the demands of the Grand Opera's regulations—rules which you think you must not dare to violate, even in a single instance.*

And it is precisely this that gives me such gloomy presentiments with regard to our beloved Freischütz. —Ah!—if you would and could but hear and see our *true* Freischütz,—you might feel the anxiety that now oppresses me, in the form of a friendly appreciation on your own part of the peculiarity of that spiritual life, which belongs to the German nation as a birthright; you would look kindly upon the silent attraction that draws the German away from the life of his large cities,—wretchedly and clumsily imitative of foreign influences, as it is,—and takes him back to nature; attracts him to the solitude of the forests, that he may there reawaken those emotions for which your language has not even a word,—but which those mystic, clear tones of our Weber explain to us as thoroughly as your exquisite decorations and enervating music must make them lifeless and irrecognizable for you.

And yet—attempt it! Try to breathe the fresh air of our forests through this strange and heavy atmosphere. I only fear that, even at the best, the unnatural mixture that results will disagree with you.

---

* It is interesting to note that the Metropolitan Opera succumbed to this same procedure when *Der Freischütz* was last revived there in 1923–24. The recitatives were by the late Artur Bodanzky, and the *Invitation to the Waltz* was again interpolated. At a previous revival, under Alfred Hertz in 1909–10, the spoken dialogue was used.—Ed.

On Franz Liszt

By Robert Schumann

Would that I could, ye distant ones and foreigners, who can scarcely hope ever to see this surpassing artist, and who therefore search out every word that is spoken or written concerning him,—would that I could give you a correct idea of him! It is more easy to speak of his outward appearance. People have often tried to picture this by comparing Liszt's head to Schiller's or Napoleon's; and the comparison so far holds good, in that extraordinary men possess certain traits in common, such as an expression of energy and strength of will in the eyes and mouth. He has some resemblance to the portraits of Napoleon as a young general—pale, thin, with a remarkable profile, the whole significance of his appearance culminating in the head. But his resemblance to the deceased Ludwig Schunke is remarkable, and this resemblance extends to their art. While listening to Liszt's playing, I have often imagined myself listening again to one I heard long before. But

163

this art is scarcely to be described. It is not this or that style of piano-forte playing; it is rather the outward expression of a daring character, to whom Fate has given, as instruments of victory and command, not the dangerous weapons of war, but the peaceful ones of art.

No matter how many great artists we may possess, or have seen pass before us during recent years, though some of them equal him in single points, all must yield to him in energy and boldness. People have been very fond of placing Thalberg in the lists beside him, and drawing comparisons. But it is only necessary to look at both heads to come to a conclusion. I remember the remark of a Viennese designer, who said, not inaptly, of his countryman's head, that it resembled "that of a handsome countess with a man's nose;" while of Liszt he observed, that "he might sit to every painter for a Grecian God." There is a similar difference in their art. Chopin stands nearer Liszt as a player, for at least he loses nothing beside him in fairylike grace and tenderness; next to him, Paganini, and, among women, Madame Malibran; from these Liszt himself acknowledges that he has learned the most.

Liszt is now probably about thirty years old.* Every one knows well that he was a child-phenomenon, how he was early transplanted to foreign lands; that his name afterwards appeared here and there among the most distinguished; that then the rumour of it occa-

* Since this visit occurred in 1840, and Liszt was born in 1811, Schumann's impression was accurate enough.—Ed.

sionally died away, until Paganini appeared, inciting the youth to new endeavours; and that he suddenly appeared in Vienna two years ago, rousing the Imperial city to enthusiasm.

Since the establishment of our paper, we have followed Liszt's career, concealing nothing that has been publicly said for or against his art, though by far the greater number of voices, especially those of all great artists, have sounded his praise. Thus he appeared among us of late, already honoured with the highest honours that can be bestowed on an artist, and his fame firmly established. It would be difficult to raise this, or to say anything new about him, though it would be easy enough to try to unsettle and injure it, as pedants and rascals are fond of doing at all times. This was lately tried here. Not from any fault of Liszt, the public had been made restless with previous announcements, and rendered ill-humoured by mistakes in the concert arrangements. A writer, notorious here for his lampoons, made use of this to attack Liszt anonymously, on account of his visit to us,—"Made with no object except to satisfy his insatiable avarice." Such vileness is unworthy of further thought.

The first concert, on the 17th, was a remarkable one. The multitudinous audience was so crowded together, that even the hall looked altered. The orchestra was also filled with listeners, and among them Liszt.

He began with the *scherzo* and *finale* of Beethoven's Pastoral Symphony. The selection was capricious enough, and on many accounts, not happy. At home, in a *tête-à-tête,* a highly-careful transcription may lead one almost to forget the orchestra; but in a large hall, in the same place where we have been accustomed to hear the symphony played frequently and perfectly by the orchestra, the weakness of the pianoforte is striking, and the more so the more an attempt is made to represent masses in their strength. A simpler arrangement, a mere sketch, would perhaps have been more effective here. Let it be understood, with all this, that we had heard the master of the instrument; people were satisfied; they had at least seen him shake his mane. To hold to the same illustration, the lion presently began to show himself more powerful. This was in a fantasia on themes by Pacini, which he played in a most remarkable manner. But I would sacrifice all the astonishing, audacious bravura that he displayed here for the sake of the magical tenderness that he expressed in the following *étude,* with the sole exception of Chopin, as I have already said, I know not one who equals him in this quality. He closed with the well-known chromatic galop; and as the applause this elicited was endless, he also played his equally well-known bravure waltz.

Fatigue and indisposition prevented the artist from giving the concert promised for the next day. In the meanwhile, a musical festival was prepared for him, that will never be forgotten by Liszt himself, or by the other persons present. The giver of the festival (F. Mendelssohn) had selected for performance some compositions yet unknown to his guest: Franz Schubert's symphony;* his own psalm, "As the hart pants"; the overture, "A calm sea and a prosperous voyage"; three choruses from "St. Paul"; and, to close with the D-minor concerto for three pianos by Sebastian Bach. This was played by Liszt, Mendelssohn, and Hiller. It seemed as though nothing had been prepared, but all improvised instantaneously. Those were three such happy musical hours as years do not always bring. At the end, Liszt played alone, and wonderfully. The assembly broke up amid the most joyful excitement, and the gaiety and happiness that sparkled in all eyes must have sufficiently attested the guests' gratitude toward the giver of a festival offered by him in homage to the artistic talents of another.

Liszt's most genial performance was yet to come— Weber's Concertstück, which he played at his second concert. Virtuoso and public seemed to be in the freshest mood possible on that evening, and the enthusiasm during and after his playing almost exceeded anything hitherto known here. Although Liszt grasped the piece from the beginning, with such force and grandeur of expression that an attack on a battlefield seemed to be in question, yet he carried this on with continually increasing power, until the passage where the player seems to stand at the summit of the orchestra leading it forward in triumph. Here indeed he resembled that great commander to whom he has been compared, and the tempestuous applause that greeted him was not unlike an adoring "Vive l'Empereur!" He then played a

* Presumably the C major.—Ed.

fantasia on themes from the "Huguenots," the "Ave Maria," and "Serenade," and, at the request of the public, the "Erlking" of Schubert. But the Concert-stück was the crown of this evening.

I do not know who originated the idea of the present of flowers handed to him at the close of the concert by a favourite songstress, but the crown was certainly not undeserved; and how spiteful, how envious a nature is necessary to disparage such a friendly attention in the way this was done by a "critic" in one of the papers here! The artist has devoted his whole life to procure for you the joy you receive from him; you know nothing of the fatigue his art has cost him; he gives you the best he has—his heart's blood, the essence of his being; and shall we then grudge him even a simple crown of flowers? But Liszt was determined not to remain a debtor. With visible delight in the enthusiastic reception he had received at his second concert, he declared himself at once ready to give one for the benefit of any charitable institution, the selection to be left to the decision of experienced persons.

So for the third time, he played again last Monday night for the benefit of the pension fund for aged or invalid musicians, though he had given a concert for the poor in Dresden the day before. The hall was completely crowded; the object of the concert, the programme, the assistance of our most famous songstress, and, above all, Liszt himself, had created the highest interest in the concert. Still fatigued with his journey and from his recent playing in concerts, Liszt arrived

in the morning, and went at once to the rehearsal, so
that he had little time to himself before the concert
hour. It was impossible for him to take any rest. I
would not leave this unmentioned: a man is not a god,
and the visible effort with which Liszt played on that
evening was but a natural consequence of what preceded the concert.

With pieces by composers residing here,—Mendelssohn, Hiller, and myself; Mendelssohn's latest concerto, *études* by Hiller, and several numbers from an
early work of mine entitled "The Carnival"—to the
astonishment of many timid virtuosos, I must state
that Liszt played these compositions almost at sight.
He had a slight former acquaintance with the *études*
and "The Carnival," but he had never seen Mendelssohn's concerto until a few days before the concert. He
was, however, so continually occupied, that he had
been unable to find time, at such short notice, for
private study. He met my doubt as to whether such
rhapsodical sketches as mine of carnival life would
make any impression on the public, with the assurance
that he hoped they would. I think he was mistaken.

Here I may perhaps be allowed to make a few observations regarding this composition, which owed its
origin to chance. The name of a city, in which a musical friend of mine lived consisted of letters belonging to the scale which are also contained in my name;
and this suggested one of those tricks that are no
longer new, since Bach gave the example. One piece
after another was completed during the carnival sea-

son of 1835, in a serious mood of mind, and under peculiar circumstances. I afterwards gave titles to the numbers, and named the entire collection "The Carnival." Though certain traits in it may please certain persons, its musical moods change too rapidly to be easily followed by a general public that does not care to be roused anew every moment.

My amiable friend did not consider this; and though he played the work with such great sympathy and geniality that it could not fail to strike a few, the masses were not excited by it. It was different with Hiller's *études,* that belong to a more recognized form; one in D flat major, another in C minor, both very tender yet characteristic, awakened warm interest. Mendelssohn's concerto was already well known through its composer's clear, masterly, reposeful playing.

As I have already observed, Liszt played these pieces almost at sight; no one will be very well able to imitate him in this. He displayed his virtuosity in its fullest force, however, in the closing piece, the "Hexameron," a cyclus of variations by Thalberg, Herz, Pixis, and Liszt himself. Everybody wondered where he found the strength to repeat half of the "Hexameron," and then his own galop, to the delight of the enraptured public. How much I hoped that he would give us some of Chopin's compositions, which he plays incomparably, with the deepest sympathy! But in his own room he amiably plays anything that is asked from him. How often have I thus listened to him in admiration and astonishment!

By Felix Mendelssohn

A LETTER TO HIS MOTHER

The turmoil of the last few weeks was overpowering.* Liszt was here for a fortnight, and caused quite a paroxysm of excitement among us, both in a good and evil sense. I consider him to be in reality an amiable warm-hearted man, and an admirable artist. That he plays with more execution than all the others, does not admit of a doubt; yet Thalberg, with his composure and within his more restricted sphere, is more perfect, taken as a virtuoso; and this is the standard which must also be applied to Liszt, for his compositions are inferior to his playing, and, in fact, are only calculated for virtuosi. A fantasia by Thalberg (especially that on the "Donna del Largo") is an accumulation of the most exquisite and delicate effects, and a continued succession of difficulties and embellishments

---

* In this letter to his mother, Mendelssohn discusses the same visit of Liszt to Leipzig treated by Schumann in the foregoing essay. It is dated March 30, 1840.—Ed.

171

that excite our astonishment; all is so well devised and so finished, carried out with such security and skill, and pervaded by the most refined taste.

On the other hand, Liszt possesses a degree of velocity and complete independence of finger, and a thoroughly musical feeling, which can scarcely be equalled. In a word, I have heard no performer whose musical perceptions, like those of Liszt, extended to the very tips of his fingers, emanating directly from them. With this power, and his enormous technicality and practice, he must have far surpassed all others, if a man's own ideas were not, after all, the chief point, and these, hitherto at least, seem denied to him, so that in this phase of art most of the great virtuosi equal, and indeed excel him.

But that he, along with Thalberg, *alone* represents the highest class of pianists of the present day, is I think undeniable. Unhappily, the manner in which Liszt has acted towards the public here has not pleased them. The whole misunderstanding is, in fact, as if you were listening to two persons disputing, who are both in the wrong, and whom you would fain interrupt at every word. As for the citizens in general, who are angry at the high prices, and do not wish to see a clever fellow prosper too much, and grumble accordingly, I don't in the least care about them; and then the newspaper discussions, explanations, and counter-explanations, criticisms and complaints, and all kinds of things are poured down on us, totally unconnected with music; so that his stay here has caused us almost as much annoyance as pleasure, though the latter was, indeed, often great beyond measure.

It occurred to me that this unpleasant state of feeling might be most effectually allayed, by people seeing and hearing him in private; so I suddenly determined to give him a *soirée* in the Gewandhaus, of three hundred and fifty persons, with orchestra, choir, mulled wine, cakes, my "Meeresstille," a Psalm, a triple concerto by Bach (Liszt, Hiller and I), choruses from "St. Paul," fantasia on "Lucia di Lammermoor," the "Erl King," the *devil and his grand-mother,"* and goodness knows what else; and all the people were delighted, and played and sang with the utmost enthusiasm, and vowed they had never passed a more capital evening; so my object was thus happily effected in a most agreeable manner.

On Robert Franz

By Robert Schumann

There is much to say regarding these *lieder* (opus 1)
by Robert Franz; * they are not isolated productions,
but bear an inward relationship to the whole development of our art during the past ten years. It is well
known that in the years 1830–34, a reaction took place
in opposition to the reigning taste. On the whole, the
struggle was not a difficult one; it was principally waged
with that empty flourish of manner that displayed itself in nearly every department of art (always except-
ing the works of Weber, Loewe, and a few others), and
especially in pianoforte music.

The first attack was made on this last; more thoughtful pictures began to take the place of mere passage
work, an influence of two masters—Beethoven and
Bach—became perceptible in these. The young musical
party grew numerous, the new life penetrated into other
branches. Franz Schubert had already worked on the

* *Neue Zeitschrift,* July 1843.

lied form, but principally in the Beethovenian manner, while the influence of Bach was more perceptible in North German song. Development was hastened by the appearance of a new school of German poetry. Eichendorff and Rückert, though they began to write before this time, had now become familiar to musicians, and Uhland and Heine were frequently set to music. Thus arose that more artistic and profound style of song, of which earlier composers could of course know nothing, since it was the new spirit of poetry reflected in music.

The songs of Robert Franz thoroughly belong to this noble new style. Hurdygurdy sing-song writing, the reciting penny verses with the same indifferences as a poem by Rückert, for example, is beginning to be estimated at its proper value and though this progress has not yet reached the mass of the public, the better class has long been aware of it. And indeed the *lied* is the only form of composition in which a remarkable improvement has taken place since Beethoven's time. If, for instance, we compare the industry which has been made use of in the songs before us to interpret the ideas of the poems almost word for word, with the negligence of the former mode of treatment, in which the poem was considered of very secondary importance; or contrast the whole harmonic construction here, with the slovenly formulas of accompaniment which earlier times found so difficult to shake off; only narrow-minded prejudice will fail to perceive this great improvement.

Robert Franz's characteristics as a *lied* composer are expressed in the preceding sentence. He desires more than well or ill sounding music; he strives to reflect the poem with lifelike profundity. He is most successful in the quietly dreamy mood, but we find in him some simple, charming traits, as in the first song, then the "Dance-song in May," and some yet more cheerful out-wellings to some of Robert Burns's texts. This double book of songs suggests the most varied pictures and feelings, and all bear a trace of melancholy. For the performance of these songs we need a poet as well as a singer; but they will please best sung when alone and at evening. A few things in them are painful to my ear, as the beginnings of the 7th and 12th songs, and the often-returning E in the last. I wish the 7th had been omitted from the collection; it seems to me too artificial in melody and harmony. The others are interesting, remarkable, often uncommonly fine. Tieck's slumber-song should have had a more richly musical close, but it is, notwithstanding, one of the happiest. It would be an endless task to describe separately the fine musical features of these songs; musicians of feeling will discover them for themselves.

These *lieder,* then, differ remarkably from others. But he who has thus commenced, must not wonder if higher things are demanded from him in future. Success in a small style often leads to one-sidedness and mannerism. We trust the young artist will protect himself from this by grasping new artistic forms, and by expressing his rich inward feelings otherwise than in

songs.* Our sympathy, however, will be with him on
any path.

* Franz wrote, however, virtually no other music.—Ed.

On Bruckner

By Hugo Wolf

Bruckner? Bruckner? Who is he? Where does he live? What can he do? * Such are the questions heard in Vienna, and especially from patrons of the subscription concerts of the Philharmonic and the Society of the Friends of Music. And if you do meet someone who is acquainted with the name he will recall that Bruckner is Professor of Music Theory at the local conservatory. Another person will add, with a triumphant glance at the semi-educated enquirer, that Bruckner is an organ virtuoso. A third music-lover will believe, a fourth will know, a fifth will even declare, and a sixth will finally swear that Bruckner is also a composer.

And the connoisseur will shake his noble head to say that Bruckner's form is not quite adroit, the amateur will complain of the confusion in Bruckner's ideas, another commentator will decry the poor instrumenta-

* An article of December 28, 1884.

178

tion, and finally, the critic will find everything terrible, and so—*basta.*

Only one other individual is left to be heard from —the conductor. The conductor approves of the composer, defends his works, and, despite criticism, proposes that Bruckner's symphonies should be played. But to whom must the conductor make the suggestion? His orchestra, his servants, so to speak. But here the lone conductor finds that he is far from having dictatorial powers. If the tribunes of the orchestra veto the decision of the conductor he may move heaven and earth to gain his ends—in vain.

(The consequences of such a situation are obvious, particularly when members of the orchestra understand as little of a composition as they do their instruments. A good soldier does not make a good general; and an orchestra player may be a technical expert on his instrument and still be unable to perform a moving, well-executed solo.)

With the conductor's defeat the last hope disappears, and Bruckner, a titan locked in battle with the gods, is forced to make himself understood by means of the piano. It is bad, but still better than not being heard at all. And if in this unfortunate situation he can be said to be lucky at all, Bruckner is lucky to have found two enthusiastic interpreters in Messrs. Lowe and Schalk. And with them Bruckner's unjust treatment at the hands of the influential music circle is somewhat ameliorated.

I mentioned that Bruckner is a titan battling with

the gods. And in truth, I cannot think of a better figure by which to paint the characteristics of this composer. For in it both praise and blame are combined.
Raw, natural powers in conflict with intellectual superiority, or, in the person of the composer, an extraordinary natural artistry, freshness, and naivete thrust
against a musical self-consciousness, intelligence, and
education—these are the principal contradictory elements in the development of this artist. If the composer
could have smoothed this antagonism he could undoubtedly achieve an importance equal to Liszt's. It is
the lack of a certain intelligence that makes Bruckner's
symphonies so difficult for us to understand, despite
their originality, freshness, strength, imagination, and
invention. In all of them there is a great Will, and tre-
mendous Force, but no satisfaction, no artistic solution.
And from this apparent extravagance of expression
there springs that characteristic formlessness of his
works. Bruckner wrestles with the idea, but lacks the
courage to point it, and then to proceed further with a
clear conscience. Thus he teeters midway between Beethoven, and the new achievements as best expressed in
the symphonic poems of Franz Liszt. Bruckner seems
to strike roots somewhere between the two, without being able to decide to which he belongs. That is his
misfortune.

I do not mean to imply that Bruckner's symphonies
are the most significant symphonic expressions since
Beethoven. They are the work of a genius, an ill-starred
genius, similar in quality to the great poetry of Grabbe.

On Bruckner

Bold, grand-scaled conceptions are common to both artists, as is a loose and formless execution of the con-
cepts. Like Grabbe, who reminds us of Shakespeare by
virtue of the riot of his fantasy and the brilliance of his
thoughts, Bruckner recalls Beethoven to us by means
of his great themes and the thoughtful uses to which
they are put. It is well worth the trouble to pay this
stormy figure more attention than he has received. It is
a shattering sight to see this extraordinary man banned
from the concert halls, this man who has first call
among contemporary composers (except Liszt, of
course) on our praises and admiration.*

* It must be remembered that Wagner had died in February
of the preceding year.

On Wagner

By Hector Berlioz

The Dresden orchestra, for a long time under the command of the Italian, Morlachi, and the illustrious composer of the *Freischütz* is conducted now by the Messrs. Reissiger and Richard Wagner.* We in Paris hardly know anything of Reissiger beyond the sweet, melancholy waltz published under the title of *Weber's Last Thought;* during my stay in Dresden one of his sacred compositions was given, which was greatly praised in my hearing. I could not add my praises; the day of the ceremony at which it was performed I was kept to my bed by cruel sufferings, and I was thus unhappily prevented from hearing it. As for the young *Kapellmeister* Richard Wagner, who lived for a long

* This is an excerpt from the fifth in a series of letters recounting Berlioz's experiences during a journey through Germany in 1841–42. This one was addressed to Henry Ernst, the celebrated violinist and composer of a concerto (F sharp minor), fancied by virtuosi.—Ed.

while in Paris without succeeding in making himself otherwise known than as the author of some articles published in the *Gazette musicale,* he exercised his authority for the first time in helping me in my rehearsals, which he did with zeal and a very good will.

The ceremony of his presentation to the orchestra and taking the oath took place the day after my arrival, and I found him in all the intoxication of a very natural joy. After having undergone in France a thousand privations and all the trials to which obscurity is exposed, Richard Wagner on coming back to Saxony, his native country, had the daring to undertake and the happiness to achieve the composition of the text and music of an opera in five acts *(Rienzi).* This work had a brilliant success in Dresden. It was soon followed by the *Flying Dutchman,* an opera in three acts, of which also he wrote both text and music. Whatever opinion one may hold of these works, it must be acknowledged that men capable of accomplishing this double literary and musical task twice with success are not common, and that M. Wagner has given enough proof of his capacity to excite interest, and rivet the attention of the world upon himself. This was very well understood by the King of Saxony; and the day that he gave his first *Kapellmeister* Richard Wagner for a colleague, thus assuring the latter's subsistence, all friends of art must have said to His Majesty what Jean Bart answered to Louis XIV, when he made him commander of a squadron: "Sire, you have done well!"

The opera of *Rienzi,* exceeding by a good deal the

length ordinarily assigned to operas in Germany, is now no longer given entire; the first two acts are given one evening and the three last the next. I only saw the second part; I could not become thoroughly enough acquainted with it, hearing it only once, to be in condition to give a final opinion; I only remember a beautiful prayer in the last act sung by *Rienzi* (Tichatschek) and a triumphal march, well modeled upon the magnificent march in *Olympie* but without servile imitation. The score of the *Flying Dutchman* seemed to me remarkable for its sombre coloring and certain stormy effects perfectly in keeping with the subject; but I could not help noticing also an abuse of the *tremolo,* which was the more regrettable that I had already been struck by it in *Rienzi,* and that it announced a certain lazy habit of mind in the author against which he is not sufficiently on guard.* The sustained *tremolo* is, of all orchestral effects, the one that one grows tired of soonest; besides, it makes no demands upon the composer's invention when it is accompanied, either above or below, by no salient idea.

Be it as it may, I repeat that we must honor the royal thought which has, so to speak, saved a young artist of precious gifts, by granting him a complete and active protection.

The administration of the Dresden theatre has neglected nothing that could add all possible brilliancy to the performance of Wagner's two works; the scenery,

* The habit was still with Wagner when he wrote *Die Walküre.*—Ed.

costumes and *mise-en-scène* approach the best things of the kind in Paris. Madame Devrient, of whom I shall take occasion to speak at greater length *apropos* of her performances in Berlin, plays the part of a young boy in *Rienzi;* this dress hardly suits the rather maternal outline of her figure.—She struck me as much more fittingly placed in the *Flying Dutchman,* in spite of some affected poses and *spoken* interjections that she feels called upon to introduce everywhere. But a pure and complete talent, which had a most vivid effect upon me, was that of Wechter, who filled the part of the cursed Dutchman. His baritone voice is one of the finest I have heard, and he uses it like a consummate singer; his voice has that unctuous, vibrating quality which has such great expressive power, whatever amount of heart and sensibility the artist throws into his singing; and Wechter possesses both these qualities to a very high degree.

By Claude Debussy

The *Société des Grandes Auditions de France* did not honour me with an invitation to listen to the recent performance of *Parsifal* at the Nouveau-Théâtre * under the director, Alfred Cortot. Alfred Cortot is the French conductor who has used to the best advantage the pantomime customary to German conductors. Like Nikisch—who, however, is Hungarian—he has a lock of hair, and that lock is in the highest degree arresting owing to the quivers of passion which agitate it on the slightest provocation. Sometimes it droops sadly and wearily in the tender passages, interposing a complete screen between Cortot and the orchestra. Then again it rears itself proudly in the martial passages. At such moments Cortot advances on the orchestra and aims a threatening baton, like a banderillero when he wants to irritate the bull. The members of the orchestra are as cool as Icelanders: they have been there before. Cortot,

* This was, of course, a concert performance. The first European stage production of *Parsifal* outside of Bayreuth was given at Zurich in April 1913. The pirated production at the Metropolitan Opera had preceded this by ten years.

like Weingartner, leans affectionately over the first violins, murmuring intimate secrets; he swoops round to the trombones, adjuring them with an eloquent gesture, that might be translated: "Now my lads! Put some go into it! Try to be supertrombones!" and the obedient trombones conscientiously do their best to swallow the brass tubes.

It is only fair to add that Cortot understands the innermost secrets of Wagner and is himself a perfect musician. He is young, his love of music is quite disinterested; and those are good reasons enough for not being too hard on him for gestures that are more decorative than useful.

To return to the *Société des Grandes Auditions,* did it intend to punish me for my Wagnerian iconoclasm by depriving me of *Parsifal?* Did it fear a subversive attitude or a bombshell? I do not know, but I should prefer to think that these private performances are designed for people whose nobility or position in high society entitles them to attend such little entertainments with a well-bred indifference to what is played. The unimpeachable distinction of the name on the programme frees them from the need of any other illumination and makes it possible to listen attentively to the latest scandal or to watch those pretty movements of the heads of women who are not listening to music. But let the *Société des Grandes Auditions* beware! They will turn Wagner's music into a fashionable at home. After all, that phase of Wagnerian art which originally imposed on his votaries costly pilgrimages and mys-

terious rites is irritating. I am well aware that this
Religion of Art was one of Wagner's favorite ideas;
and he was right, for such a formula is excellent for
capturing and holding the imagination of an audience;
but it has miscarried by becoming a kind of Religion of
Luxury, excluding perforce many people who are richer
in enthusiasm than in cash. The *Société des Grandes
Auditions,* by carrying on these traditions of exclusiveness seems to me doomed to end in that detestable
thing, the art of fashionable society. When Wagner
was in a good humor he liked to maintain that he would
never be so well understood in France. Was he refer-
ring to aristocratic performances only? I do not think
so. King Louis II of Bavaria was already annoying him
enough with questions of arbitrary etiquette; and Wagner's proud sensitiveness was too acute to miss the fact
that true fame comes solely from the masses and not
from a more or less gilded and exclusive public. It is
to be feared that these performances, directed avowedly
at the diffusion of Wagnerian art, may serve only to
alienate the sympathy of the masses: a cunning trick
to make it unpopular. I do not mean that the performances will hasten a final eclipse; for Wagner's art can
never completely die. It will suffer that inevitable de-
cay, the cruel brand of time on all beautiful things; yet
noble ruins must remain, in the shadow of which our
grandchildren will brood over the past splendour of
this man who, had he been a little more human, would
have been altogether great.

In *Parsifal,* the final effort of a genius which compels

our homage, Wagner tried to drive his music on a looser rein and let it breathe more freely. We have no longer the distraught breathlessness that characterises Tristan's morbid passion or Isolde's wild screams of frenzy; nor yet the grandiloquent commentary on the inhumanity of Wotan.

Nowhere in Wagner's music is a more serene beauty attained than in the prelude to the third act of *Parsifal* and in the entire Good Friday episode; although it must be admitted that Wagner's peculiar conception of human nature is also shown in the attitude of certain characters in this drama. Look at Amfortas, that melancholy Knight of the Grail, who whines like a shop girl and whimpers like a baby. Good heavens! A Knight of the Grail, a king's son, would plunge his spear into his own body rather than parade a guilty wound in doleful melodies for three acts! As for Kundry, that ancient rose of hell, she has furnished much copy for Wagnerian literature; and I confess I have but little affection for such a sentimental draggle-tail. Klingsor is the finest character in *Parsifal:* a quondam Knight of the Grail, sent packing from the Holy Place because of his too pronounced views on chastity. His bitter hatred is amazing; he knows the worth of men and scornfully weighs the strength of their vows of chastity in the balance. From this it is quite obvious that this crafty magician, this old gaol-bird, is not merely the only human character but the only moral character in this drama, in which the falsest moral and religious ideas are set forth, ideas of which the youthful Parsifal is the heroic and insipid champion.

Here in short is a Christian drama in which nobody is willing to sacrifice himself, though sacrifice is one of the highest of the Christian virtues! If Parsifal recovers his miraculous spear, it is thanks to old Kundry, the only creature actually sacrificed in the story: a victim twice over, once to the diabolical intrigues of Klingsor and again to the sacred spleen of a Knight of the Grail. The atmosphere is certainly religious, but why have the incidental children's voices such sinister harmonies? Think for a moment of the childlike candor that would have been conveyed if the spirit of Palestrina had been able to dictate its expression.

The above remarks only apply to the poet whom we are accustomed to admire in Wagner and have nothing to do with the musical beauty of the opera, which is supreme. It is incomparable and bewildering, splendid and strong. Pasifal is one of the loveliest monuments of sound ever raised to the serene glory of music.

By Peter Tchaikovsky

I have seen Wagner's *Walküre*.* The performance was excellent. The orchestra surpassed itself; the best singers did all within their powers—and yet it was wearisome. What a Don Quixote is Wagner! He expends his whole force in pursuing the impossible, and all the time, if he would but follow the natural bent of his extraordinary gift, he might evoke a whole world of musical beauties. In my opinion Wagner is a symphonist by nature. He is gifted with genius which has wrecked itself upon his tendencies; his inspiration is paralysed by theories which he has invented on his own account, and which, *nolens volens,* he wants to bring into practice. In his efforts to attain *reality, truth,* and *rationalism* he lets *music* slip quite out of sight, so that in his four latest operas it is, more often than not, conspicuous by its absence. I cannot call that music which consists of kaleidoscopic, shifting phrases, which succeed each other without a break and never come to a

* This estimate of Wagner was written by Tchaikovsky from Vienna in 1877 to his "Beloved Friend" Nadejda von Meck.

close, that is to say, never give the ear the least chance
to rest upon musical form. Not a single broad, rounded
melody, nor yet one moment of repose for the singer!
The latter must always pursue the orchestra, and be
careful never to lose his note, which has no more importance in the score than some note for the fourth
horn.

But there is no doubt Wagner is a wonderful symphonist. I will just prove to you by one example how
far the symphonic prevails over the operatic style in his
operas. You have probably heard his celebrated *Wal-
kürenritt?* What a great and marvellous picture! How
we actually seem to see these fierce heroines flying on
their magic steeds amid thunder and lightning! In the
concert-room this piece makes an extraordinary impression. On the stage, in view of the cardboard rocks, the
canvas clouds, and the soldiers who run about very
awkwardly in the background—in a word, seen in this
very inadequate theatrical heaven which makes a poor
pretence of realising the illimitable realms above, the
music loses all its powers of expression. Here the stage
does not enhance the effect, but acts rather like a wet
blanket.

Finally I cannot understand, and never shall, why
the *Nibelungen* should be considered a literary masterpiece. As a national saga—perhaps, but as a libretto—
distinctly not!

Wotan, Brünnhilda, Fricka, and the rest are all so
impossible, so little human, that it is very difficult to
feel any sympathy with their destinies. And how little

life! For three whole hours Wotan lectures Brünnhilda upon her disobedience. How wearisome! And with it all, there are many fine and beautiful episodes of a purely symphonic description.

[Despite his disagreement with Wagner's artistic principles and his slight feeling for the end to which that composer aspired, Tchaikovsky was no less able to dismiss him from his thoughts than were Brahms and Verdi. Two years later, from Brailov, Tchaikovsky wrote again to von Meck:]

Yesterday I began to study the score of *Lohengrin.* I know you are no great admirer of Wagner, and I, too, am far from being a desperate Wagnerite. I am not very sympathetic to Wagnerism as a principle. Wagner's personality arouses my antipathy,* yet I must do justice to his great musical gift. This reaches its climax in *Lohengrin,* which will always remain the crown of all his works. After *Lohengrin,* began the deterioration of his talent, which was ruined by his diabolical vanity. He lost all sense of proportion, and began to overstep all limits, so that everything he composed after *Lohengrin* became incomprehensible, impossible music which has no future. What chiefly interests me in *Lohengrin* at present is the orchestration. In view of the work which lies before me, I want to study this score very closely, and decide whether to adopt some of his methods of instrumentation. His mastery is extraor-

* It may be recalled that Wagner did not receive Tchaikovsky when the latter called on him at Bayreuth in 1876.—Ed.

dinary, but, for reasons which would necessitate technical explanations, I have not borrowed anything from him. Wagner's orchestration is too symphonic, too overloaded and heavy for vocal music. The older I grow, the more convinced I am that symphony and opera are in every respect at the opposite poles of music. Therefore the study of *Lohengrin* will not lead me to change my style, although it has been interesting and of negative value.

[And again, from Berlin, in 1882 (also to von Meck):]

Yesterday *Tristan und Isolde* (which I had never seen) was being given at the Opera, so I decided to remain another day. The work does not give me any pleasure, although I am glad to have heard it, for it has done much to strengthen my previous views of Wagner, which—until I had seen all his works performed —I felt might not be well grounded. Briefly summed up, this is my opinion: in spite of his great creative gifts, in spite of his talents as a poet, and his extensive culture, Wagner's services to art—and to opera in particular—have only been of a negative kind. He has proved that the older forms of opera are lacking in all logical and aesthetic *raison d'être*. But if we may no longer write opera on the old lines, are we obliged to write as Wagner does? I reply, *Certainly not*. To compel people to listen for four hours at a stretch to an endless symphony which, however rich in orchestral colour, is wanting in clearness and directness of thought; to keep singers all these hours singing melodies which have no independent existence, but are merely notes that belong to this symphonic music (in spite of lying very high these notes are often lost in the thunder of the orchestra), this is certainly not the ideal at which contemporary musicians should aim.

Wagner has transferred the centre of gravity from the stage to the orchestra, but this is an obvious absurdity, therefore his famous operatic reform—viewed apart from its negative results—amounts to nothing. As regards the dramatic interest of his operas, I find them very poor, often childishly naive. But I have never been quite so bored as with *Tristan und Isolde*. It is an endless void, without movement, without life, which cannot hold the spectator, or awaken in him any true sympathy for the characters on the stage. It was evident that the audience—even though Germans—were bored, but they applauded loudly after each act. How can this be explained? Perhaps by a patriotic sympathy for the composer, who actually devoted his whole life to singing the praise of Germanism.

[Though this would suggest that Tchaikovsky had uttered his last word on Wagner and Wagnerism, he writes in another letter to von Meck, two years later:]

I have realised two intentions since I came here (Plestchievo): the study of two works hitherto unknown to me—Moussorgsky's *Khovanshchina* and Wagner's *Parsifal*. In the first I discovered what I expected: pretensions to realism, original conceptions and methods, wretched technique, poverty of invention, occasionally clever episodes, amid an ocean of harmonic absurdities and affectations. . . .

Parsifal leaves an entirely opposite impression. Here we are dealing with a great master, a genius, even if he has gone somewhat astray. His wealth of harmony is so luxuriant, so vast, that at length it becomes fatiguing, even to a specialist. What then must be the feelings of an ordinary mortal who has wrestled for three hours with this flow of complicated harmonic combinations? To my mind Wagner has killed his colossal creative genius with *theories*. Every preconceived theory chills his incontestable creative impulse. How could Wagner abandon himself to inspiration, while he believed he was grasping some particular theory of music-drama, or musical truth, and, for the sake of this, turned from all that, according to his predecessors, constituted the strength and beauty of music? If the singer may not *sing,* but—amid the deafening clamour of the orchestra—is expected to declaim a series of set and colourless phrases, to the accompaniment of a gorgeous, but disconnected and formless symphony, is that opera?

What really astounds me, however, is the. seriousness with which this philosophising German sets the most inane subjects to music. Who can be touched, for instance, by *Parsifal,* in which, instead of having to deal with men and women similar in temperament and feeling to ourselves, we find legendary beings, suitable perhaps for a ballet, but not for a music drama? I cannot understand how anyone can listen without laughter, or without being bored, to those endless monologues in which Parsifal, or Kundry, and the rest bewail their misfortunes. Can we sympathise with them? Can we love or hate them? Certainly not; we remain aloof from their passions, sentiments, triumphs, and misfortunes. But that which is unfamiliar to the human heart should never be the source of musical inspiration. . . .

On "The Five"

By Peter Tchaikovsky

The young Petersburg composers are very gifted,* but they are all impregnated with the most horrible presumptuousness and a purely amateur conviction of their superiority to all other musicians in the universe.

The one exception, in later days, has been Rimsky-Korsakov. He was also an 'auto-dictator' like the rest, but recently he has undergone a complete change. By nature he is very earnest, honorable, and conscientious. As a very young man he dropped into a set which first solemnly assured him he was a genius, and then proceeded to convince him that he had no need to study, that academies were destructive to all inspiration and dried up creative activity. At first he believed all this. His earliest compositions bear the stamp of striking ability and a lack of theoretical training. The circle to which he belonged was a mutual admiration society. Each member was striving to imitate the work of

* From a letter to von Meck, December 1878.

198

another, after proclaiming it as something very wonderful. Consequently the whole set suffered from one-sidedness, lack of individuality, and mannerisms. Rimsky-Korsakov is the only one among them who discovered, five years ago, that the doctrines preached by this circle had no sound basis, that their mockery of the schools and the classical masters, their denial of authority and of the masterpieces, was nothing but ignorance.

I possess a letter dating from that time which moved me very deeply. Rimsky-Korsakov was overcome by despair when he realized how many unprofitable years he had wasted, and that he was following a road which led nowhere. He began to study with such zeal that the theory of the schools soon became to him an indispensable atmosphere. During one summer he achieved innumerable exercises in counterpoint and sixty-four fugues, ten of which he sent me for inspection. From contempt for the schools, Rimsky-Korsakov suddenly went over to the cult of musical technique. Shortly after this appeared his symphony and also his quartet. Both works are full of obscurities and—as you will justly observe—bear the stamp of dry pedantry. At present he appears to be passing through a crisis, and it is hard to predict how it will end. Either he will turn out a great master, or be lost in contrapuntal intricacies.

C. Cui is a gifted amateur. His music is not original, but graceful and elegant; it is too coquettish—'made up'—so to speak. At first it pleases, but soon satiates us. That is because Cui's specialty is not music, but fortification, upon which he has to give a number of lectures in the various military schools in St. Petersburg. He himself once told me he could only compose by picking out his melodies and harmonies as he sat at the piano. When he hit upon some pretty idea, he worked it up in every detail, and this process was very lengthy, so that his opera *Ratcliff*, for instance, took him ten years to complete. But, as I have said, we cannot deny that he has talent of a kind—and at least taste and instinct.

Borodin—aged fifty—Professor of Chemistry at the Academy of Medicine, also possesses talent, a very great talent, which however has come to nothing for the want of teaching, and because blind fate has led him into the science laboratories instead of a vital musical existence. He has not as much taste as Cui, and his technique is so poor that he cannot write a bar without assistance.

With regard to Moussorgsky, as you very justly remark, he is 'used up.' His gifts are perhaps the most remarkable of all, but his nature is narrow and he has no aspirations towards self-perfection. He has been too easily led away by the absurd theories of his set and the belief in his own genius. Besides which his nature is not of the finest quality, and he likes what is coarse, unpolished, and ugly. He is the exact opposite of the distinguished and elegant Cui.

Moussorgsky plays with his lack of polish—and even seems proud of his want of skill, writing just as it comes to him, believing blindly in the infallibility of his genius. As a matter of fact his very original talent flashes forth now and again.

Balakirev is the greatest personality of the entire circle. But he relapsed into silence before he had accomplished much. He possesses a wonderful talent which various fatal hindrances have helped to extinguish. After having proclaimed his agnosticism rather widely, he suddenly became 'pious.' Now he spends all his time in church, fasts, kisses the relics—and does very little else. In spite of his great gifts, he has done a great deal of harm. For instance, he it was who ruined Korsakov's early career by assuring him he had no need to study. He is the inventor of all the theories of this remarkable circle which unites so many undeveloped, falsely developed, or prematurely decayed, talents.

These are my frank opinions upon these gentlemen. What a sad phenomenon! So many talents from which—with the exception of Rimsky-Korsakov—we can scarcely dare to hope for anything serious. But this is always our case in Russia: vast forces which are impeded by the fatal shadow of a Plevna from taking the open field and fighting as they should. But all the same, these forces exist. Thus Moussorgsky, with all his ugliness, speaks a new idiom. Beautiful it may not be, but it is new. We may reasonably hope that Russia will one day produce a whole school of strong men who will open up new paths in art.

On Brahms

By Peter Tchaikovsky

The Concerto [Violin Concerto, Op. 77] of Brahms
does not please me better than any other of his works.*
He is certainly a great musician, even a master, but, in
his case, his mastery overwhelms his inspiration. So
many preparations and circumlocutions for something
which ought to come and charm us at once—and nothing does come, but boredom. His music is not warmed
by any genuine emotion. It lacks poetry, but makes
great pretensions to profundity. These depths contain
nothing: they are void. Take the opening of the Concerto, for instance. It is an introduction, a preparation
for something fine; an admirable pedestal for a statue;
but the statue is lacking, we only get a second pedestal
piled upon the first. I do not know whether I have

* This is a longer expression of opinion about Brahms than
Tchaikovsky ordinarily confided to von Meck (the letter was
written from Rome in March, 1880), but thoroughly characteristic.

properly expressed the thoughts, or rather feelings, which Brahms's music awakens in me. I mean to say that he never expresses anything, or, when he does, he fails to express it fully. His music is made up of fragments of some indefinable *something*, skilfully welded together. The design lacks definite contour, color, life.

But I must simply confess that, independent of any definite accusation, Brahms, as a musical personality, is antipathetic to me. I cannot abide him. Whatever he does—I remain unmoved and cold. It is a purely instinctive feeling.

In his diary of October 1886, Tchaikovsky writes:

Played Brahms. It irritates me that this self-conscious mediocrity should be recognised as a genius. In comparison with him, Raff was a giant, not to speak of Rubinstein, who was a much greater man. And Brahms is so chaotic, so dry and meaningless!

However, his personal impression of Brahms (to be found in the diary of a tour to Germany in 1888), was not unfavorable:

Brahms is rather a short man, suggests a sort of amplitude, and possesses a very sympathetic appearance. His fine head—almost that of an old man—recalls the type of a handsome, benign, elderly Russian priest. His features are certainly not characteristic of German good looks, and I cannot conceive why some learned ethnographer (Brahms himself told me this after I had spoken of the impression his appearance made upon me) chose to reproduce his head on the first page of his books as being highly characteristic of German features. A certain softness of outline, pleasing curves, rather long and slightly grizzled hair, kind grey eyes, and a thick beard, freely sprinkled with white—all this recalled at once the type of pure-bred Great Russian so frequently met with among our clergy. Brahms's manner is very simple, free from vanity, his humor jovial, and the few hours spent in his society left me with a very agreeable recollection.

Later in the same year, Tchaikovsky replied to a letter of the Grand Duke Constantine Constantinovitch:
As regards Brahms, I cannot at all agree with your Highness. In the music of this master (it is impossible to deny his mastery) there is something dry and cold which repulses me. He has very little melodic invention. He never speaks out his musical ideas to the end. Scarcely do we hear an enjoyable melody, than it is engulfed in a whirlpool of unimportant harmonic progressions and modulations, as though the special aim of the composer was to be unintelligible. He excites and irritates our musical senses without wishing to satisfy them, and seems ashamed to speak the language which goes straight to the heart. His depth is not real: *c'est voulu.* He has set before himself, once and for all, the aim of trying to be profound, but he has only attained to an appearance of profundity. The gulf is void.

It is impossible to say that the music of Brahms is weak and insignificant. His style is invariably lofty. He does not strive after mere external effects. He is never

On Brahms

trivial. All he does is serious and noble, but he lacks the chief thing—beauty. Brahms commands our respect. We must bow before the original purity of his aspirations. We must admire his firm and proud attitude in the face of triumphant Wagnerism; but to love him is impossible. I, at least, in spite of much effort, have not arrived at it . . . I will own that certain early works (the Sextet in B♭) please me far more than those of a later period, especially the symphonies, which seem to me indescribably long and colourless . . .

Many Brahms lovers (Bülow,* among others) predicted that some day I should see clearer, and learn to appreciate beauties which do not as yet appeal to me. This is not unlikely, for there have been such cases. I do not know the *German Requiem* well. I will get it and study it. Who knows?—perhaps my views on Brahms may undergo a complete revolution.†

* Tchaikovsky was similarly impervious to von Bülow's enthusiasm for the youthful Richard Strauss. Writing to his brother Modeste from Berlin in January 1888, he said: "Bülow has taken him up just now, as formerly he took up Brahms and others. To my mind such an astounding lack of talent, united to such pretentiousness, never before existed."
† They didn't.—Ed.

On Conducting

By Hector Berlioz

Music appears to be the most exacting of all the arts, the most difficult to cultivate, and that of which the productions are most rarely presented in a condition which permits an appreciation of their real value, a clear view of their physiognomy, or discernment of their real meaning and true character.* Of producing artists, the composer is almost the only one, in fact, who depends upon a multitude of intermediate agents, either intelligent or stupid, devoted or hostile, active or inert, capable—from first to last—of contributing to the brilliancy of his work, or of disfiguring it, misrepresenting it, and even destroying it completely.

Singers have often been accused of forming the most dangerous of these intermediate agents; but in my opinion, without justice. The most formidable, to my think-

* The dissertation of which this is an excerpt was added to Berlioz's classic work on *Instrumentation* when it was re-issued in 1856.—Ed.

ing, is the conductor of the orchestra. A bad singer can spoil only his own part; while an incapable or malevolent conductor ruins all. Happy, also, may that composer esteem himself when the conductor into whose hands he has fallen is not at once incapable and inimical. For nothing can resist the pernicious influence of this person. The most admirable orchestra is then paralyzed, the most excellent singers are perplexed and rendered dull; there is no longer any vigour or unity; under such direction the noblest daring of the author appears extravagance, enthusiasm beholds its soaring flight checked, inspiration is violently brought down to earth, the angel's wings are broken, the man of genius passes for a madman or an idiot, the divine statue is precipitated from its pedestal and dragged in the mud. And, what is worse, the public, and even auditors endowed with the highest musical intelligence, are reduced to the impossibility (if a new work be in question, and they are hearing it for the first time) of recognizing the ravages perpetrated by the orchestral conductor—of discovering the follies, faults, and crimes he commits. If they clearly perceive certain defects of execution, not he but his victims are in such cases made responsible. If he have caused the chorus-singers to fail in taking up a point in a finale, if he have allowed a discordant wavering to take place between the choir and the orchestra, or between the extreme sides of the instrumental body, if he have absurdly hurried a movement, if he have allowed it to linger unduly, if he have interrupted a singer before the end of a phrase they exclaim: "The singers are detestable! The orchestra has no firmness; the violins have disfigured the principal design; everybody has been wanting in vigor and animation; the tenor was quite out, he did not know his part; the harmony is confused; the author is no accompanist; the voices are—'' &c., &c.

Except in listening to great works already known and esteemed, intelligent hearers can hardly distinguish the true culprit, and allot to him his due share of blame; but the number of these is still so limited that their judgment has little weight; and the bad conductor—in presence of the public who would pitilessly hiss a *vocal accident* of a good singer—reigns, with all the calm of a bad conscience, in his baseness and inefficiency. Fortunately, I here attack an exception; for the malevolent orchestral conductor—whether capable or not—is very rare.

The orchestral conductor full of goodwill, but incapable, is, on the contrary, very common. Without speaking of innumerable mediocrities directing artists who, frequently, are much their superiors, an author, for example, can scarcely be accused of conspiring against his own works. Yet how many are there who, fancying they are able to conduct, innocently injure their best scores!

Beethoven, it is said, more than once ruined the performance of his symphonies; which he would conduct, even at the time when his deafness had become almost complete. The musicians, in order to keep together, agreed at length to follow the slight indications of time which the concertmeister (first violin-player) gave them; and not to attend to Beethoven's conducting-stick. Moreover, it should be observed, conducting a symphony, an overture or any other composition whose movements remain continuous, vary little, and contain few nice gradations, is child's play in comparison with conducting an opera, or like work, where there are recitatives, airs, and numerous orchestral designs preceded by pauses of irregular length.

The example of Beethoven, which I have just cited, leads me at once to say that if the direction of an orchestra appears to me very difficult for a blind man, it is indisputably impossible to a deaf one, whatever may have been his technical talent before losing his sense of hearing.

The orchestral conductor should *see* and *hear;* he should be *active* and *vigorous,* should know the *composition* and the *nature* and *compass* of the instruments, should be able to *read* the score, and possess—besides the especial talent of which we shall presently endeavor to explain the constituent qualities—other almost indefinable gifts, without which an invisible link cannot establish itself between him and those he directs; the faculty of transmitting to them his feeling is denied him, and thence power, empire, and guiding influence completely fail him. He is then no longer a conductor, a director, but a simple beater of the time—supposing he knows how to beat it, and divide it, regularly.

The performers should feel that he feels, comprehends, and is moved: then his emotion communicates itself to those whom he directs, his inward fire warms them, his electric glow animates them, his form of impulse excites them; he throws around him the vital irradiations of musical art. If he be inert and frozen on the contrary, he paralyzes all about him, like those floating masses of the polar seas the approach of which is perceived through the sudden cooling of the atmosphere.

His task is a complicated one. He has not only to conduct, in the spirit of the author's intentions, a work with which the performers have already become acquainted, but he has also to give them this acquaintance when the work in question is new to them. He has to criticize the errors and defects of each during the rehearsals, and to organize the resources at his disposal in such a way as to make the best use he can of them with the utmost promptitude. For, in the majority of European cities nowadays, musical artisanship is so ill distributed, performers so ill paid, and the necessity of study so little understood, that *economy of time* should be reckoned among the most imperative requisites of the orchestral conductor's art.

Let us now see what constitutes the mechanical part of this art.

The power of *beating the time,* without demanding very high musical attainments, is nevertheless sufficiently difficult to secure, and very few persons really possess it. The signs that the conductor should make— although generally very simple—nevertheless become complicated, under certain circumstances, by the divison and even the subdivision of the time of the bar.

The conductor is, above all, bound to possess a clear idea of the principal points and character of the work of which he is about to superintend the performance or study; in order that he may, without hesitation or mistake, at once determine the time of each movement desired by the composer. If he have not had the opportunity of receiving his instructions directly from the composer or if the *times* have not been transmitted to him by tradition, he must have recourse to the indications of the metronome, and study them well; the majority of composers, nowadays, taking the precaution to write them at the head, and in the course of, their pieces. I do not mean to say by this that it is necessary to imitate the mathematical regularity of the metronome; all music so performed would become of freezing stiffness, and I even doubt whether it would be possible to observe so flat a uniformity during a certain number of bars. But the metronome is none the less excellent to consult in order to know the original time, and its chief alterations.*

If the conductor possess neither the author's instructions, tradition, nor metronome indications,—which frequently happens in the ancient master-pieces, written at a period when the metronome was not invented,—he has no other guide than the vague terms employed to

* Wagner's opinion on this point provides an interesting contrast. See page 220.—Ed.

designate the time to be taken, and his own instinct, his feeling—more or less distinguishing, more or less just —of the author's style. We are compelled to admit that these guides are too often insufficient and delusive. Of this we have proof in seeing how old operas are given in towns where the traditional mode of performance no longer exists. In ten different kinds of time, there will always be at least four taken wrongly. I once heard a chorus of *Iphigenia in Tauride* performed in a German theatre *allegro assai, two in the bar,* instead of *allegro non troppo, four in the bar;* that is to say, exactly twice too fast. Examples might be multiplied of such disasters, occasioned either by the ignorance or the carelessness of conductors of orchestras; or else by the real difficulty which exists for even the best-gifted and most careful men to discover the precise meaning of the Italian terms used as indications of the time to be taken. Of course no one can be at a loss to distinguish a Largo from a Presto. If the Presto be two in a bar, a tolerably sagacious conductor, from inspection of the passages and melodic designs contained in the piece, will be able to discern the degree of quickness intended by the author. But if the Largo be four in a bar, of simple melodic structure and containing but few notes in each bar, what means has the hapless conductor of discovering the true time? And in how many ways might he not be deceived? The different degrees of slowness that might be assigned to the performance of such a Largo are very numerous; the individual feeling of the orchestral conductor must then become the sole authority;

and, after all, it is the author's feeling, not his, which is in question. Composers therefore ought not to neglect placing metronome indications in their works; then orchestral conductors will be bound to study them closely. The neglect of this study on the part of the latter is an act of dishonesty.

By Richard Wagner

Looking back upon my earliest youth I remember to
have had unpleasant impressions from performances of
classical orchestral music.* At the piano or whilst reading a score, certain things appeared animated and expressive, whereas, at a performance, they could hardly
be recognised, and failed to attract attention. I was
puzzled by the apparent flabbiness of Mozartian melody
(*cantilena*) which I had been taught to regard as so
delicately expressive. Later in life I discovered the reasons for this, and I have discussed them in my report
on a "German music school to be established at Munich,"
to which I beg to refer readers who may be interested
in the subject. Assuredly, the reasons lie in the want of
a proper conservatorium of German music—a *conservatory,* in the strictest sense of the word, in which the
traditions of the *classical masters' own* style of execution are preserved in practice—which, of course, would
imply that the masters should once, at least, have had a

* Originally published in the *Neu Zeitschrift für Musik* and
the *New-Yorker Musik-zeitung* in 1869.

214

chance personally to supervise performances of their
works in such a place. Unfortunately German culture
has missed all such opportunities; and if we now wish
to become acquainted with the spirit of a classical composer's music, we must rely on this or that conductor,
and upon his notion of what may, or may not, be the
proper *tempo* and style of execution.

In the days of my youth, orchestral pieces at the celebrated Leipzig Gewandhaus Concerts were not conducted at all; they were simply played through under
the leadership of Conzertmeister Mathai, like overtures
and *entr'actes* at a theatre. At least there was no "dis-
turbing individuality," in the shape of a conductor!
The principal classical pieces which presented no particular technical difficulties were regularly given every
winter; the execution was smooth and precise; and the
members of the orchestra evidently enjoyed the annual
recurrence of their familiar favorites.

With Beethoven's Ninth Symphony alone they could
not get on, though it was considered a point of honor
to give that work every year. I had copied the score for
myself, and made a pianoforte arrangement for two
hands; but I was so much astonished at the utterly confused and bewildering effect of the Gewandhaus performance that I had lost courage, and gave up the study
of Beethoven for some time. Later I found it instructive to note how I came to take true delight in performances of Mozart's instrumental works: it was when I
had a chance to conduct them myself, and when I could

indulge my feelings as to the expressive rendering of Mozart's *cantilena*.

I received a good lesson at Paris in 1839, when I heard the orchestra of the Conservatoire rehearse the enigmatical Ninth Symphony. The scales fell from my eyes: I came to understand the value of *correct* execution and the secret of a good performance. The orchestra had learned to look for Beethoven's *melody* in every bar—that melody which the worthy Leipzig musicians had failed to discover; and the orchestra *sang* that melody. *This was the secret.*

Habeneck, who solved the difficulty, and to whom the great credit for this performance is due, was not a conductor of special genius. Whilst rehearsing the symphony, during an entire winter season, he had felt it to be incomprehensible and ineffective (would German conductors have confessed as much?) but he persisted throughout a second and a third season, until Beethoven's new *melos* * was understood, and correctly rendered by each member of the orchestra. Habeneck was a conductor of the old stamp; *he* was the master—and everyone obeyed him. I cannot attempt to describe the beauty of this performance. However, to give an idea of it, I will select a passage by the aid of which I shall endeavor to show the reason why Beethoven is so difficult to render as well as the reason for the indifferent success of German orchestras when confronted by such difficulties. Even with first-class orchestras I

* Wagner's inclusive term for the continuous, pervasive melodic line of a work.—Ed.

have never been able to get the passage in the first
movement:

performed with such equable perfection as I then
(thirty years ago) heard it played by the musicians
of the Paris Orchestre du Conservatoire. Often in later
life have I recalled this passage, and tried by its aid
to enumerate the desiderata in the execution of orchestral music; it comprises *movement* and *sustained*
tone, with a *definite degree of power.* The masterly
execution of this passage by the Paris orchestra consisted in the fact that they played it *exactly* as it is written. Neither at Dresden, nor in London when in after
years I had occasion to prepare a performance of the
symphony, did I succeed in getting rid of the annoying
irregularity which arises from the change of bow and
change of strings. Still less could I suppress an involuntary accentuation as the passage ascends; musicians,
as a rule, are tempted to play an ascending passage with
an increase of tone, and a descending one with a de-

crease. With the fourth bar of the above passage we invariably got into a crescendo so that the sustained G flat of the fifth bar was given with an involuntary yet vehement accent, enough to spoil the peculiar tonal significance of that note.

The composer's intention is clearly indicated; but it remains difficult to prove to a person whose musical feelings are not of a refined sort, that there is a great gap between a commonplace reading, and the reading meant by the composer; no doubt both readings convey a sense of dissatisfaction, unrest, longing—but the *quality* of these, the true sense of the passage, cannot be conveyed unless it is played as the master imagined it, and as I have not hitherto heard it given except by the Parisian musicians in 1839.

In connection with this I am conscious that the impression of dynamical monotony (if I may risk such an apparently senseless expression for a difficult phenomenon) together with the unusually varied and ever irregular movement of intervals in the ascending figure entering on the prolonged G flat to be sung with such infinite delicacy, to which the G natural answers with equal delicacy, initiated me as by magic to the incomparable mystery of the spirit. Keeping my further practical experience in view, I would ask how did the musicians of Paris arrive at so perfect a solution of the difficult problem? By the most conscientious diligence. They were not content with mutual admiration and congratulation nor did they assume that difficulties must disappear before them as a matter of course. French musicians in the main belong to the Italian school; its influence upon them has been beneficial inasmuch as they have thus been taught to approach music mainly through the medium of the human voice. The French idea of playing an instrument well is to be able to *sing* well upon it. And (as already said) that superb orchestra *sang* the symphony.

The possibility of its being well sung implies that the *true tempo* had been found: and this is the second point which impressed me at the time. Old Habeneck was not the medium of any abstract aesthetical inspiration—he was devoid of "genius": *but he found the right tempo whilst persistently fixing the attention of his orchestra upon the* melos *of the symphony.*

The right comprehension of the melos *is the sole guide to the right tempo;* these two things are inseparable: the one implies and qualifies the other.

As a proof of my assertion that the majority of performances of instrumental music with us are faulty it is sufficient to point out that *our conductors so frequently fail to find the true tempo because they are ignorant of singing.* I have not yet met with a German capellmeister or musik-director, who, be it with good or bad voice, can really sing a melody. These people look upon music as a singularly abstract sort of thing, an amalgam of grammar, arithmetic and digital gymnastics; to be an adept in which may fit a man for a mastership at a conservatory or musical gymnasium; but it does not follow from this that he will be able to put life and soul into a musical performance.

Wagner

The whole duty of a conductor is comprised in his ability always to indicate the right *tempo*. His choice of *tempi* will show whether he understands the piece or not. With good players, again, the true *tempo* induces correct phrasing and expression will induce the conception of the true *tempo*.

This, however, is by no means so simple a matter as it appears. Older composers probably felt so, for they are content with the simplest general indications. Haydn and Mozart made use of the term "andante" as the mean between allegro and adagio, and thought it sufficient to indicate a few gradations and modifications of these terms.

Sebastian Bach, as a rule, does not indicate *tempo* at all, which in a truly musical sense is perhaps best. He may have said to himself: whoever does not understand my themes and figures, and does not feel their character and expression, will not be much the wiser for an Italian indication of *tempo*.*

Let me be permitted to mention a few facts which concern me personally. In my earlier operas I gave detailed directions as to the *tempi,* and indicated them (as I thought) accurately, by means of the metronome. Subsequently, whenever I had occasion to protest against a particularly absurd *tempo*, in *Tannhäuser* for instance, I was assured that the metronome had been consulted and carefully followed. In my later works I omitted the metronome and merely described the main *tempi* in

* This succinct sentence conveys one of the most discerning comments in all of Wagner's prose writing.—Ed.

general terms, paying, however, particular attention to the various modifications of *tempo*. It would appear that general directions also tend to vex and confuse capellmeisters, especially when they are expressed in plain German words. Accustomed to the conventional Italian terms these gentlemen are apt to lose their wits when, for instance, I write *mässig* (moderate).

Not long ago a capellmeister complained of that term which I employed in the score of *Das Rheingold;* the music (it was reported) lasted exactly two hours and a half at rehearsals under a conductor whom I had personally instructed: whereas at the performances and under the beat of the official capellmeister, it lasted fully three hours! (according to the report of the *Allgemeine Zeitung*). Wherefore, indeed, did I write *mässig?*

To match this I have been informed that the overture to *Tannhäuser,* which, when I conducted it at Dresden, used to last twelve minutes, now lasts twenty. No doubt I am here alluding to thoroughly incompetent persons who are particularly shy of *alla breve* time, and who stick to their correct and normal crotchet beats, four in a bar, merely to show they are present and conscious of doing something. Heaven knows how such "quadrupeds" find their way from the village church to our opera theatres. But "dragging" is not a characteristic of the elegant conductors of these latter days; on the contrary they have a fatal tendency to hurry and to run away with the *tempi. This tendency to hurry* is so characteristic a mark of our entire musical life latterly, that I propose to enter into some details with regard to it.

Robert Schumann once complained to me at Dresden that he could not enjoy the Ninth Symphony at the Leipzig Gewandhaus Concerts because of the quick *tempi* Mendelssohn chose to take, particularly in the first movement. I have, myself, only once been present at a rehearsal of one of Beethoven's symphonies when Mendelssohn conducted: the rehearsal took place at Berlin, and the symphony was No. 8 (in F major). I noticed that he chose a detail here and there—almost at random—and worked at it with a certain obstinacy, until it stood forth clearly. This was so manifestly to the advantage of the detail that I could not but wonder why he did not take similar pains with other nuances. For the rest, this incomparably bright symphony was rendered in a remarkably smooth and genial manner. Mendelssohn himself once remarked to me, with regard to conducting, that he thought most harm was done by taking a *tempo* too slow; and that, on the contrary, he always recommended quick *tempi* as being less detrimental. Really good execution, he thought, was at all times a rare thing, but shortcomings might be disguised if care was taken that they should not appear very prominent; and the best way to do this was "to get over the ground quickly." This can hardly have been a casual view, accidentally mentioned in conversation. The master's pupils must have received further and more detailed instruction; for subsequently I have, on various occasions, noticed the consequences of that maxim, "take quick *tempi*," and have, I think, discovered the reasons which may have led to its adoption.

I remembered it well, when I came to lead the orchestra of the Philharmonic Society in London, 1855. Mendelssohn had conducted the concerts during several seasons, and the tradition of his readings was carefully preserved. It appears likely that the habits and peculiarities of the Philharmonic Society suggested to Mendelssohn his favorite style of performance—certainly it was admirably adapted to meet their wants. An unusual amount of instrumental music is consumed at these concerts; but as a rule, each piece is rehearsed only once. Thus in many instances I could not avoid letting the orchestra follow its traditions, and so I became acquainted with a style of performance which called up a lively recollection of Mendelssohn's remarks.

The music gushed forth like water from a fountain, there was no arresting it, and every *allegro* ended as an undeniable *presto*. It was troublesome and difficult to interfere; for when correct *tempo* and proper modifications of these were taken, the defects of style which the flood had carried along or concealed became painfully apparent. The orchestra generally played *mezzo forte;* no real *forte,* no real *piano* was attained. Of course in important cases I took care to enforce the reading I thought the true one, and to insist upon the right *tempo.* The excellent musicians did not object to this, on the contrary they showed themselves sincerely glad of it; the public also approved, but the critics were annoyed, and continued so to browbeat the directors of the society that the latter actually requested me to permit the second movement of Mozart's Symphony in E flat to be played in the flabby and colorless way they had been accustomed to—and which, they said, even Mendelssohn himself had sanctioned.

The fatal maxims came to the front quite clearly when I was about to rehearse a symphony by a very amiable elderly contrapuntist, Mr. Potter, if I mistake not. The composer approached me in a pleasant way, and asked me to take the andante rather quickly as he feared it might prove tedious. I assured him that his andante, no matter how short its duration might be, would inevitably prove tedious if it was played in a vapid and inexpressive manner; whereas if the orchestra could be got to play the very pretty and ingenious theme, as I felt confident he meant it and as I now sang it to him, it would certainly please. Mr. Potter was touched; he agreed, and excused himself, saying that latterly he had not been in the habit of reckoning upon this sort of orchestral playing. In the evening, after the andante, he joyfully pressed my hand.

I have often been astonished at the singularly slight sense for *tempo* and execution evinced by leading musicians. I found it impossible, for instance, to communicate to Mendelssohn what I felt to be a perverse piece of negligence with regard to the *tempo* of the third movement in Beethoven's Symphony in F major, No. 8. This is one of the instances I have chosen out of many to throw light upon certain dubious aspects of music amongst us.

We know that Haydn in his principal later symphonies used the form of the minuet as a pleasant link between the adagio and the final allegro, and that he thus was induced to increase the speed of the movement considerably, contrary to the character of the true minuet. It is clear that he incorporated the *Ländler*, particularly in the trio—so that with regard to the *tempo,* the designation "menuetto" is hardly appropriate, and was retained for conventional reasons only. Nevertheless, I believe Haydn's minuets are generally taken too quickly: * undoubtedly the minuets of Mozart's symphonies are. This will be felt very distinctly if, for instance, the menuetto in Mozart's Symphony in G minor, and still more that of his Symphony in C major be played a little slower than at the customary pace. It will be found that the latter minuet, which is usually hurried, and treated almost as a presto will now show an amiable, firm and festive character, in contrast with which, the trio, with its delicately sustained

 is

is reduced, as usually given, to an empty hurry-scurry. Now Beethoven, as is not uncommon with him, meant to write a true minuet in his F major Symphony; he

* As a generalization, this is still a valid criticism of most performances of Haydn minuets.—Ed.

places it between the two main allegro movements as a sort of complementary antithesis to an allegretto scherzando which precedes it, and to remove any doubt as to his intentions regarding the *tempo,* he designates it *not* as a menuetto but as a *tempo di menuetto.* This novel and unconventional characterization of the two middle movements of a symphony was almost entirely overlooked: the allegretto scherzando was taken to represent the usual andante, the *tempo di menuetto,* the familiar scherzo, and, as the two movements thus interpreted seemed rather paltry, and none of the usual effects could be got with them, our musicians came to regard the entire symphony as a sort of accidental *hors d'oeuvre* of Beethoven's muse—who after the exertions with the A major Symphony had chosen "To take things rather easily."

Accordingly after the allegretto scherzando, the time of which is invariably "dragged" somewhat, the *tempo di menuetto* is universally served up as a refreshing *Ländler,* which passes the ear without leaving any distinct impression. Generally, however, one is glad when the tortures of the trio are over. This loveliest of idylls is turned into a veritable monstrosity by the passage in triplets for the violoncello; which if taken at the usual quick pace, is the despair of violoncellists, who are worried with the hasty staccato across the strings and back again, and find it impossible to produce anything but a painful series of scratches. Naturally, this difficulty disappears as soon as the delicate melody of the horns and clarinets is taken at the proper *tempo;* these instruments are thus relieved from the special difficulties pertaining to them, and which, particularly with the clarinet, at times render it likely to produce a "quack" even in the hands of skilful players. I remember an occasion when all the musicians began to breathe at ease on my taking this piece at the true moderate pace: then the humorous *sforzato* of the basses and bassoons

at once produced an intelligible effect; the short *crescendi* became clear, the delicate *pianissimo* close was effective, and the gentle gravity of the returning principal movement was properly felt. Now, the late Capellmeister Reissiger, of Dresden, once conducted this symphony there, and I happened to be present at the performance together with Mendelssohn; we talked about the dilemma just described, and its proper solution, concerning which I told Mendelssohn that I believed I had convinced Reissiger who had promised that he would take the *tempo* slower than usual. We listened. The third movement began and I was terrified on hearing precisely the old Ländler *tempo;* but before I could give vent to my annoyance Mendelssohn smiled, and pleasantly nodded his head, as if to say "Now it's all right! Bravo!" So my terror changed to astonishment. Reissiger, for reasons which I shall discuss presently, may not have been so very much to blame

227

for persisting in the old *tempo;* but Mendelssohn's indifference, with regard to this queer artistic contre-
temps, raised doubts in my mind whether he saw any
distinction and difference in the case at all. I fancied
myself standing before an abyss of superficiality, a veritable void.

Soon after this had happened with Reissiger, the very
same things took place with the same movement of the
Eighth Symphony at Leipzig. The conductor, in the latter case, was a well-known successor of Mendelssohn
at the Gewandhaus Concerts.* He also had agreed with
my views as to the *tempo di menuetto,* and had invited
me to attend a concert at which he promised to take it
at the proper *moderato* pace. He did not keep his word
and offered a queer excuse: he laughed, and confessed
that he had been disturbed with all manner of adminis-
trative business, and had only remembered his promise
after the piece had begun; naturally he could not then
alter the *tempo,* etc. The explanation was sufficiently
annoying. Still I could, at least, flatter myself that I had
found somebody to share my views as to the difference
between one *tempo* and another. I doubt, however,
whether the conductor could be fairly reproached with
a want of forethought and consideration; unconsciously,
perhaps, he may have had a very good reason for his
"forgetfulness." It would have been very indiscreet to
risk a change of *tempo* which had not been rehearsed.
For the orchestra, accustomed to play the piece in a
quick *tempo,* would have been disturbed by the sudden

* Ferdinand Hiller.

imposition of a more moderate pace; which, as a matter of course, demands a totally different style of playing.

We have now reached an important and decisive point, an appreciation of which is indispensable if we care to arrive at a satisfactory conclusion regarding the execution of classical music. Injudicious *tempi* might be defended with some show of reason inasmuch as a factitious style of delivery has arisen in conformity with them, and to the uninitiated such conformity of style and *tempo* might appear as a proof that all was right. The evil, however, is apparent enough, if only the right *tempo* is taken, in which case the false style becomes quite unbearable.

To illustrate this, in the simplest possible way, let us take the opening of the C minor Symphony.

Usually the fermata of the second bar is left after a slight rest; our conductors hardly make use of this fermata for anything else than to fix the attention of their men upon the attack of the figure in the third bar. In most cases the note E flat is not held any longer than a *forte* produced with a careless stroke of the bow will last upon the stringed instruments. Now, suppose the voice of Beethoven was heard from the grave admonishing a conductor: "Hold my fermata firmly, terribly! I did not write fermatas in jest, or because I was at a loss how to proceed; I indulge in the fullest, the most sustained tone to express emotions in my adagio; and I use this full and firm tone when I want it in a passionate allegro as a rapturous or terrible spasm. Then the very life blood of the tone shall be extracted to the last drop. I arrest the waves of the sea, and the depths shall be visible; or, I stem the clouds, disperse the mist, and show the pure blue ether and the glorious eye of the sun. For this I put fermatas, sudden long sustained notes in my allegro. And now look at my clear thematic intention with the sustained E flat after the three stormy notes, and understand what I meant to say with other such sustained notes in the sequel."

Suppose a conductor was to attempt to hold the fermata as here directed, what would be the result? A miserable failure. After the initial power of the bow of the stringed instruments had been wasted, their tone would become thin and thinner, ending in a weak and timid *piano:* for (and here is one of the results of indifferent conducting) our orchestras nowadays hardly know what is meant by *equally sustained tone.* Let any conductor ask any orchestral instrument, no matter which, for a full and prolonged *forte,* and he will find the player puzzled, and will be astonished at the trouble it takes to get what he asks for.

Yet *tone sustained with equal power* is the basis of all expression, with the voice as with the orchestra: the manifold modifications of the power of tone, which constitute one of the principal elements of musical expression, rest upon it. Without such basis an orchestra will produce much noise but no power. And this is one of the first symptoms of the weakness of most of our orchestral performances. The conductors of the day care little about a sustained *forte,* but they are particularly fond of an *exaggerated piano.* Now the strings produce the latter with ease, but the wind instruments, particularly the wood winds, do not. It is almost impossible to get a delicately sustained *piano* from wind instruments.

The players, flutists particularly, have transformed their formerly delicate instruments into formidable tubes. French oboists, who have preserved the pastoral character of their instrument, and our clarinetists, when they make use of the "Echo effect," are the exceptions.

This drawback, which exists in our best orchestras, suggests the question: why, at least, do not conductors try to equalize matters by demanding a somewhat fuller *piano* from the strings? But the conductors do not seem to notice any discrepancy.

To a considerable extent the fault lies not so much with the wind instruments, as in the character of the *piano* of the strings; for we do not possess a *true piano,* just as we do not possess a *true forte;* both are wanting in fullness of tone—to attain which our stringed instruments should watch the tone of the winds. Of course it is easy enough to produce a buzzing vibration by gently passing the bow over the strings; but it requires great artistic command of the breath to produce a delicate and pure tone upon a wind instrument. Players of stringed instruments should copy the full-toned *piano* of the best winds, and the latter, again, should endeavor to imitate the best vocalists.

The sustained soft tone here spoken of, and the sustained powerful tone mentioned above, are the two poles of orchestral expression.

But what about orchestral execution if neither the one nor the other is properly forthcoming? Where are the modifications of expression to come from if the very means of expression are defective? Thus the Mendelssohnian rule of "getting over the ground" suggested a happy expedient; conductors gladly adopted the maxim, and turned it into a veritable dogma; so that, nowadays, attempts to perform classical music correctly are openly denounced as heretical!

I am persistently returning to the question of *tempo* because, as I said above, this is the point at which it becomes evident whether a conductor understands his business or not.

Obviously the proper pace of a piece of music is determined by the particular character of the rendering it requires; the question, therefore, comes to this: does the sustained tone, the vocal element, the *cantilena* predominate, or the rhythmical movement (figuration)? The conductor should lead accordingly.

The adagio stands to the allegro as the sustained tone stands to the *rhythmical movement*. The sustained tone regulates the tempo adagio; here the rhythm is, as it were, dissolved in pure tone, the tone *per se* suffices for the musical expression. In a certain delicate sense it may be said of the pure adagio that it cannot be taken too slow. A rapt confidence in the sufficiency of pure musical speech should reign here; the *languor* of feeling grows to ecstasy; that which in the allegro was expressed by changes of figuration, is now conveyed by means of variously inflected tone. Thus the least change of harmony may call forth a sense of surprise; and again, the most remote harmonic progressions prove acceptable to our expectant feelings.

None of our conductors are courageous enough to take an adagio in this manner; they always begin by looking for some bit of figuration, and arrange their *tempo* to match. I am, perhaps, the only conductor who has ventured to take the adagio section of the third movement of the Ninth Symphony at the pace proper to its peculiar character. This character is distinctly contrasted with that of the alternating andante in triple time; but our conductors invariably contrive to obliterate the difference, leaving only the rhythmical change between square and triple time. This movement (assuredly one of the most instructive in the present respect), finally (in the section in twelve-eight time), offers a conspicuous example of the breaking up of the pure adagio by the more marked rhythms of an independent accompaniment, during which the *cantilena* is steadily and broadly continued. In this section we may recognize, as it were, a fixed and consolidated reflex of the adagio's tendency towards infinite expansion; there, limitless freedom in the expression of sound, with fluctuating, yet delicately regulated movement; here, the firm rhythm of the figurated accompaniments, imposing the new regulation of a steady and distinct pace—in the consequences of which, when fully developed, we have got the law that regulates the movement of the allegro in general.

We have seen that sustained tone with its modification is the basis of all musical execution. Similarly the adagio developed, as Beethoven has developed it in the third movement of his Ninth Symphony, may be taken as the basis of all regulations as to musical time. In a certain delicate sense, the allegro may be regarded as the final result of a refraction of the pure adagio character by the more restless moving figuration. On careful examination of the principal motives of the allegro it will be found that the melody derived from the adagio predominates. The most important allegro movements of Beethoven are ruled by a predominant melody which exhibits some of the characteristics of the adagio; and in this wise Beethoven's allegros receive the *emotional sentimental* significance which distinguishes them from the earlier naïve species of allegro. However, Beethoven's

234

On Conducting

and Mozart's

or:

are not far asunder. And with Mozart, as with Beethoven, the exclusive character of the allegro is only felt when the figuration gets the upper hand of the melody; that is, when the reaction of the rhythmical movement against the sustained tone is entirely carried out. This is particularly the case in those final movements which have grown out of the rondo, and of which the finales to Mozart's Symphony in E flat, and to Beethoven's in A, are excellent examples. Here the purely rhythmical movement, so to speak, celebrates its orgies; and it is consequently impossible to take these movements too quickly. But whatever lies between these two extremes *is subject to the laws of mutual relationship and interdependence; and such laws cannot be too delicately and variously applied,* for they are fundamentally identical with the laws which modify all conceivable nuances of the sustained tone . . . execution are more carefully attended to, etc. But it is a very different thing to allow the necessity for reticence, and for the suppression of certain personal characteristics, to be converted into a

principle for the treatment of our art! Germans are stiff
and awkward when they want to appear mannerly: *but
they are noble and superior when they grow warm.*
And are we to suppress our fire to please those reticent
persons? In truth, it looks as though they expected us
to do so.

In former days, whenever I met a young musician
who had come in contact with Mendelssohn, I learnt
that the master had admonished him not to think of
effect when composing, and to avoid everything that
might prove meretriciously impressive. Now, this was
very pleasant and soothing advice: and those pupils
who adopted it and remained true to the master, have
indeed produced neither "impression nor meretricious
effect"; only, the advice seemed to me rather too negative, and I failed to see the value of that which was
positively acquired under it. I believe the entire teaching of the Leipzig Conservatorium was based upon
some such negative advice, and I understand that young
people there have been positively pestered with warn-
ings of a like kind; whilst their best endeavors met
with no encouragement from the masters unless their
taste in music fully coincided with the tone of the or-
thodox psalms. The first result of the new doctrine,
and the most important for our investigations, came to
light in the execution of classical music. Everything
here was governed by the fear of exaggeration *(etwa
in das Drastische zu fallen)*. I have, for instance, hitherto not found any traces that those later pianoforte
works of Beethoven in which the master's peculiar

On Conducting

style is best developed, have actually been studied and played by the converts to that doctrine.

For a long time I earnestly wished to meet with someone who could play the great sonata in B flat (Op. 106) as it should be played. At length my wish was gratified—but by a person who came from a camp wherein those doctrines do *not* prevail. Franz Liszt, also, gratified my longing to hear Bach. No doubt Bach has been assiduously cultivated by Liszt's opponents, they esteem Bach for teaching purposes, since a smooth and mild manner of execution apparently accords better with his music than "modern effect" or Beethovenian strenuousness *(Drastik)*.

I once asked one of the best-reputed older musicians, a friend and companion of Mendelssohn (whom I have already mentioned *à propos* of the *tempo di menuetto* of the eighth symphony *), to play the eighth prelude and fugue from the first part of "Das Wohltemperirte Clavier" (E flat minor), a piece which has always had a magical attraction for me.† He very kindly complied, and I must confess that I have rarely been so much taken by surprise. Certainly, there was no trace here of sombre German gothicism and all that old-fashioned stuff: under the hands of my friend, the piece ran along the keyboard with a degree of "Greek serenity" that left me at a loss whither to turn; in my innocence I deemed myself transported to a *neo-helenic*

* Ferdinand Hiller.

† I.e., Prelude VIII, from Part I of Bach's Forty-eight Preludes and Fugues.

synagogue, from the musical *cultus* of which all old testamentary accentuations had been most elegantly eliminated. This singular performance still tingled in my ears, when at length I begged Liszt for once to cleanse my musical soul of the painful impression; he played the fourth Prelude and Fugue (C sharp minor). Now, I knew what to expect from Liszt at the piano; but I had not expected anything like what I came to hear from Bach, though I had studied him well; I saw how study is eclipsed by genius. By his rendering of this single fugue of Bach's, Liszt revealed Bach to me; so that I henceforth knew for certain what to make of Bach, and how to solve all doubts concerning him. I was convinced, also, that *those* people know *nothing* of Bach; and if anyone chooses to doubt my assertion, I answer: "request him to play a piece of Bach's."

I would like further to question any member of that musical temperance society, and, if it has ever been his lot to hear Liszt play Beethoven's great B flat Sonata, I would ask him to testify honestly whether he had before really known and understood that sonata. I, at least, am acquainted with a person who was so fortunate; and who was constrained to confess that he had not before understood it. And to this day, who plays Bach, and the great works of Beethoven, in public, and compels every audience to confess as much? a member of that "school for temperance?" No! it is Liszt's chosen successor, Hans von Bülow.

So much for the present on this subject. It might prove interesting to observe the attitude these reticent gentlemen take up with regard to performances such as Liszt's and Bülow's.

The successes of their policy, to which they are indebted for the control of public music in Germany, need not detain us; but we are concerned in an examination of the curious religious development within their congregation. In this respect the earlier maxim, "beware of effect"—the result of embarrassment and cautious timidity—has now been changed from a delicate rule of prudence and security to a positively aggressive dogma. The adherents of this dogma hypocritically look askance if they happen to meet with a true man in music. They pretend to be shocked, as though they had come across something improper. The spirit of their shyness, which originally served to conceal their own impotence, now attempts the defamation of other people's potence. Defamatory insinuations and calumny find ready acceptance with the representatives of German Philistinism, and appear to be at home in that mean and paltry state of things which, as we have seen, environs our musical affairs.

The principal ingredient, however, is an apparently judicious caution in presence of that which one happens to be incapable of, together with detraction of that which one would like to accomplish one's self. It is sad, above all things, to find a man so powerful and capable as Robert Schumann concerned in this confusion, and in the end to see his name inscribed on the banner of the new fraternity. The misfortune was that Schumann in his later days attempted certain tasks for which he was not qualified. And it is a pity to see that portion of his work, in which he failed to reach the mark he had set himself, raised as the insignia of the latest guild of musicians. A good deal of Schumann's early endeavor was most worthy of admiration and sympathy, and it has been cherished and nurtured by us (I am proud here to rank myself with Liszt's friends) in a more commendable and commending way than by his immediate adherents. The latter, well aware that Schumann had herein evinced true productivity, knowingly kept these things in the background, perhaps because they could not play them in an effective way. On the other hand, certain works of Schumann conceived on a larger and bolder scale, and in which the limits of his gifts become apparent are now carefully brought forward.* The public does not exactly like these works, but their performance offers an opportunity to point out how commendable a thing it is to "make no effect." Finally, a comparison with the works of Beethoven in his third period (played as they play them) comes in opportunely.

Certain later, inflated *(schwülstig)* and dull productions of R. Schumann, which simply require to be played smoothly *(glatt herunter gespielt)* are confounded with Beethoven; and an attempt is made to show that they agree in spirit with the rarest, boldest and most profound achievements of German music!

* Such as the overtures to "Faust," "Die Braut von Messina," "Julius Caesar"; the "Balladen," "Das Glück von Edenhall," "Des Sänger Fluch," "Vom Pagen und der Königstochter," etc.

On Conducting

Thus Schumann's shallow bombast is made to pass for the equivalent of the inexpressible purport of Beethoven—but always with the reservation that strenuous eccentricity such as Beethoven's is hardly admissible; whereas, vapid emptiness *(das gleichgiltig nichtssagende)* is right and proper: a point at which Schumann properly played, and Beethoven improperly rendered, are perhaps comparable without much fear of misunderstanding! Thus these singular defenders of musical chastity stand towards our great classical music in the position of eunuchs in the Grand-Turk's Harem; and by the same token German Philistinism is ready to entrust them with the care of music in the family—since it is plain that anything ambiguous is not likely to proceed from that quarter.

But now what becomes of our great and glorious German music? It is the fate of our music that really concerns us. We have little reason to grieve if, after a century of wondrous productivity, nothing particular happens to come to light for some little time. But there is every reason to beware of suspicious persons who set themselves up as the trustees and conservators of the "true German spirit" of our inheritance.

Regarded as individuals, there is not much to blame in these musicians; most of them compose very well. Herr Johannes Brahms once had the kindness to play a composition of his own to me—a piece with very serious variations—which I thought excellent, and from which I gathered that he was impervious to a joke. His performance of other pianoforte music at a concert gave me less pleasure. I even thought it impertinent that the friends of this gentleman professed themselves unable to attribute anything beyond "extraordinary technical power" to "Liszt and his school," whilst the execution of Herr Brahms appeared so painfully dry, inflexible and wooden. I should have liked to see Herr Brahms's technique anointed with a little of the oil of Liszt's school; an ointment which does not seem to issue spontaneously from the keyboard, but is evidently got from a more ethereal region than that of mere "technique." To all appearances, however, this was a very respectable phenomenon: only it remains doubtful how such a phenomenon could be set up in a natural way as the Messiah, or at least the Messiah's most beloved disciple; unless, indeed, an affected enthusiasm for mediaeval wood-carvings should have induced us to accept those stiff wooden figures for the ideals of ecclesiastical sanctity. In any case we must protest against any presentation of our great warm-hearted Beethoven in the guise of such sanctity. If *they* cannot bring out the difference between Beethoven whom they do not comprehend and therefore pervert, and Schumann, who, for very simple reasons, *is* incomprehensible, they shall, at least, not be permitted to assume that no difference exists.

I have already indicated sundry special aspects of this sanctimoniousness. Following its aspirations a little further we shall come upon a new field, across which our investigation on and about conducting must now lead us.

On the Claque

By Hector Berlioz

A very flat modern opera is played.*

An *habitué* of the parquet-stalls, who seemed deeply interested in the readings and stories of the musicians on previous evenings, leans over into the orchestra and addresses me: "Sir, you commonly live in Paris, do you not?" "Yes, sir, I even live there uncommonly, and often more than I could wish." "In that case you must be familiar with the singular dialect spoken there, and which your papers also use sometimes. Will you please explain to me what they mean, when in describing certain occurrences that seem to be pretty frequent at dramatic performances, they talk about the Romans?" "Yes," say several musicians at once, "what is meant by that word in France?" "Why, gentlemen, you ask

---

* This is the seventh of Berlioz's 'Evenings in the Orchestra', originally published in 1852. Its modernity and appropriateness remain amazing today, save if one recalls that two things have not changed—the operas and the audience.—Ed.

me for no less than a course of Roman history." "Well, why not?" "I fear that I have not the talent of being brief." "Oh, if that is all, the opera is in four acts, and we are with you up to eleven o'clock."

So, to bring myself at once into relations with the great men of this history, I will not go back to the sons of Mars, nor to Numa Pompilius; I will jump with my feet well under me over the kings, the dictators, and the consuls; and yet I must entitle the first chapter of my history:

DE VIRIS ILLUSTRIBUS ROMAE.

Nero—(you see that I pass without transition to the time of the emperors), Nero having formed a corporation of men whose duty it was to applaud him when he sang in public, the name of *Romans* is given in France to-day to professional applauders, vulgarly called *claqueurs,* or bouquet-throwers, and in general to all undertakers of success and enthusiasm. There are several kinds.

The mother who courageously calls everybody's attention to the wit and beauty of her daughter, who is moderately beautiful and very silly; that mother who, in spite of her extreme love for her child, will make up her mind at the soonest possible moment to a cruel separation and place her in the arms of a husband, is a Roman.

The author who, foreseeing the need he will be in next year of the praise of a critic whom he detests, vehemently sings the praises of that same critic on every occasion, is a Roman.

The critic who is little enough of a Spartan to be caught in that clumsy trap becomes a Roman in his turn.

The husband of the cantatrice who . . . you understand. But the vulgar Romans, the crowd, the Roman people, in a word is especially composed of those men whom Nero was the first to enlist. They go in the evening to the theatres, and even elsewhere, to applaud, under the direction of a leader and his lieutenants, the artists and works that that leader has pledged himself to uphold.

There are many ways of applauding.

The first, as you all know, consists in making as much noise as possible by striking one hand against the other. And in this first way there are varieties and different shades: the tip of the right hand struck against the palm of the left produces a sharp, reverberating sound that most artists prefer; both hands struck together, on the contrary, have a dull and vulgar sonority; it is only pupil *claqueurs* in their first year, or barbers' apprentices that applaud so.

The gloved *claqueur* dressed like a dandy, stretches his arms affectedly out of his box and claps slowly, almost without noise, and for the eye merely; he thus says to the whole house: 'See! I condescend to applaud.'

The enthusiastic *claqueur* (for there are such) claps quick, loud, and long; his head turns to the right and

245

left during this applause; then, these demonstrations not being enough, he stamps, he cries: Bravô! Bravô! (note well the circumflex over the *o*) or 'Bravà!' (that one is learned, he has frequented the Italiens, he knows the difference between masculine and feminine) and redoubles his clamor in the ratio that the cloud of dust raised by his stamping increases in density.

The *claqueur* disguised as an old gentleman of property, or as a colonel, strikes the floor with the end of his cane with a paternal air, and in moderation.

The violinist-*claqueur*, for we have many artists in the Paris orchestras, who either to pay their court to the director of the theatre, or their conductor, or to some beloved and powerful cantatrice, enlist for the time being in the Roman army; the violinist-*claqueur*, I say, taps the body of his violin with the back of his bow. This applause, rarer than the other kinds, is consequently more sought after. Unfortunately, cruel disenchantments have taught the gods and goddesses that they can hardly ever tell when the applause of the violins is ironical or serious. Hence the anxious smile of the divinities when they receive this homage.

The kettle-drummer applauds by beating his drums; which does not happen once in fifteen years.

The Roman ladies applaud sometimes with their gloved hands, but their influence has its full effect only when they cast their bouquets at the feet of the artist they uphold. As this sort of applause is rather expensive, it is commonly the nearest relation, the most intimate friend of the artist, or the artist himself who bears the expense. So much is given to the flower-throwers for their flowers, and so much for their enthusiasm; besides, a man or a nimble boy must be paid to go behind the scenes after the first shower of flowers, pick them up and bring them back to the Roman ladies in the stage-boxes, who use them a second and often a third time.

We have also the sensitive Roman, who weeps, has nervous attacks, faints away. A very rare species, nearly extinct, closely related to the family of the giraffes.

But to confine ourselves to the study of the Roman people, properly so called, here is how and under what conditions they work:

Given a man who, either from the impulse of a natural vocation, or by long and arduous studies, has succeeded in acquiring a real talent as a Roman: he goes to the director of a theatre and says to him pretty much as follows: 'Sir, you are at the head of a dramatic enterprise the strong and weak points of which are known to me; you have as yet nobody to direct the *success;* intrust me with that; I offer you 20,000 francs down, and 10,000 francs per annum.' 'I want 30,000 francs down,' the director usually answers. 'Ten thousand francs ought not to stand in the way of our bargain; I will bring them to-morrow.' 'You have my word. I shall require a hundred men for ordinary occasions, and at least five hundred for first performances and important first appearances.' 'You shall have them, and more too.' "

'What!' said one of the musicians, interrupting me,

'is it the director that is payed! . . . I always thought it was the other party!' Yes, sir, those offices are bought, like the business of an exchange, or the practice of a lawyer or a notary.

When he once holds his *commission,* the head of the bureau of success, the emperor of the Romans, easily recruits his army among hair-dressers' apprentices, commercial travelers, cab-drivers *on foot,* * poor students, aspirants to the supernumerariat etc., etc., who have a passion for the theatre. He usually chooses a place of meeting for them, which is some obscure cafe, or a drinking place near to the centre of operations. There he counts them, gives them his instructions and tickets to the pit, or the third gallery, for which the poor devils pay thirty or forty sous, or less, according to the round of the theatrical ladder their establishment is on. The lieutenants alone always have free tickets. On great days they are paid by their chief. It even happens when a new work is to be *made to foam up from the bottom* (if it costs the direction of the theatre a great deal of money) that the chief not only does not find enough paying Romans, but cannot even find any devoted soldiers ready to give battle for the love of art. He is then obliged to pay the complement of his troupe,

* When a cab-driver has incurred the displeasure of the Prefect of Police, the latter forbids him to work at his trade of coachman for two or three weeks, in which case the unlucky fellow does not make anything, and does not, certainly, drive in a carriage. He is on foot. At such times he often enlists in the Roman infantry.—(Author's note.)

and to give each man as much as three francs and a glass of brandy.

But in that case the emperor, on his part, does not only receive pit-tickets; it is bank-notes that fall into his pocket, and in almost incredible numbers. One of the artists who is to appear in the new piece wishes to be *supported* in an exceptional manner; he offers a few tickets to the emperor. The latter puts on his coldest look, and pulling a handful of square bits of paper from his pocket: 'You see,' says he, 'that I do not want for them. What I want this evening is men, and to get them I must pay for them.' The artist takes the hint, and slips a scrap of five hundred francs into Caesar's hand. The superior of the actor who has thus looked out for himself is not long in hearing of this piece of generosity; then the fear of not being *cared for* in proportion to his merit, considering the extraordinary *care* that is to be taken of his second, makes him offer the undertaker of successes a real note of 1,000 francs, and sometimes more. And so on from the head to the foot of the *dramatis personae*. You understand now why and how the director of the theatre is paid by the director of the *claque* and how easy it is for the latter to make money.

The first great Roman that I knew at the Opera in Paris was called Auguste: the name is a lucky one for a Caesar. I have rarely seen more imposing majesty than his. He was a good prince, nevertheless; and an *habitué* of the pit, as I was then, I was often the object of his benevolence. Besides, my fervor in applauding spontaneously Gluck and Spontini, Madame Branchu and Dérivis, gained for me his particular esteem. Having brought out at that time my first score (a high-mass) at the Church of Saint-Roch, the old *dévotés*, the leaser of chairs, the man who passes around the holy water, the beadle and all the loungers of the quarter showed themselves very well satisfied, and I had the simplicity to think I had had a success at the very most; I was not long in finding it out. Seeing me again two days after that performance: 'Well!' said the emperor Auguste to me, 'So you came out at Saint-Roch day before yesterday? Why in the devil didn't you let me know of it beforehand? We should have all been there.' 'Ah! are you so fond of sacred music as that?' 'Why no, what an idea! but we would have *warmed you up well.*' 'How so? but you cannot applaud in church.' 'You cannot applaud, no; but you can cough, and blow your nose, and hitch your chair, and scrape with your feet, and say: "Hm! Hm!" and raise your eyes to heaven; all that sort of thing, hey! we would have made you *foam up* a bit; an *entire success* just like a fashionable preacher.'

Two years later I again forgot to notify him when I gave my first concert at the Conservatoire, but Auguste came, notwithstanding, with two of his aids-de-camp; and in the evening when I re-appeared in the pit at the Opera, he gave me his mighty hand, saying in paternal accents that carried conviction with them (in French of course): 'Tu Marcellus eris!'

(At this point Bacon, the viola, nudges his neighbor with his elbow and asks him softly what those three words mean. 'I don't know,' answers the other. 'It is from Virgil,' says Corsino, the first violin, who has heard the question and answer. 'It means: "You shall be Marcellus!" ' 'Well . . . what is the good of being Marcellus?' 'Not being a fool, be quiet!')

But the masters of the *claque* are not very fond, in general, of such ebullient amateurs as I was; they profess a distrust that amounts to antipathy for such adventurers, *condottieri,* lost children of enthusiasm, who come in all giddiness and *without rehearsals,* to applaud in their ranks. One day of a first performance at which there was to be, to use the Roman phrase, a *famous pull,* that is to say, great difficulty for Auguste's soldiers in conquering the public, I had happened to sit down on a bench in the pit that the emperor had marked on his plan of operations as belonging by rights exclusively to himself. I had been there a good half hour under the hostile glances of all my neighbors, who seemed to be asking themselves how to get rid of me, and I was asking myself with a certain anxiety, in spite of the purity of my conscience, what I could have done to those officers, when the emperor Auguste, rushing into the midst of his staff, came to tell me, speaking with a certain sharpness but without violence (I have already said that he was my patron) : 'My dear sir, I am obliged to disturb you; you cannot stay there.' 'Why not?' 'Well because! . . . it is impossible; you are in the middle of my first line, and you *cut me in two.'* I hastened, you may believe, to leave the field free for this great tactician.

251

Any other stranger, mistaking the urgencies of the position, would have resisted the emperor, and thus compromised the success of his combinations. Hence the opinion, founded on a long series of learned observations, an opinion openly professed by Auguste and his whole army: *the public is of no use in a theatre; it is not only of no use, but it spoils everything. As long as the public comes to the Opéra, the Opéra will not get on.* The directors in those days called him a madman when he uttered these proud words. Great Auguste! He did not dream that, in a few years after his death, such brilliant justice would be done to his doctrines! His lot was that of all men of genius, to be misunderstood by their contemporaries, and taken at an advantage by their successors.

No, never did a more intelligent and worthy dispenser of glory sit enthroned under the chandelier of a theatre.

In comparison with Auguste, he who now reigns at the Opéra is but a Vespasian, a Claudius. His name is David. And who would give him the title of emperor? Nobody. His flatterers dare to call him king at the very most, on account of his name solely.

The illustrious chief of the Romans at the Opéra-Comique is Albert; but in speaking of him, as of his old namesake, they call him Albert the Great.

He was the first to put Auguste's daring theory in practice, by pitilessly excluding the public from first performances. On those days, if we except critics, who also for the most part belong in one way or another *viris illustribus urbis Romae,* the house is now filled from top to bottom with claqueurs.

It is to Albert the Great that we owe the touching custom of recalling all the actors at the end of a new piece. King David was quick to imitate him in this; and, emboldened by the success of this first improvement, he added that of recalling the tenor as many as three times in an evening. A god who should be recalled like a simple mortal only once at the end of a state performance, would *get into an oven.* Hence it is followed that if David, in spite of all his efforts, could not obtain more than this slim result for a generous tenor, his rivals of the Théâtre-Français and the Opéra-Comique would laugh at him the next day, saying: 'David *warmed up the oven* yesterday.' I will give an explanation of these Roman technicalities by and by. Unfortunately, Albert the Great, tired of power, no doubt, saw fit to lay down his sceptre. In giving it into the hands of his obscure successor, he would willingly have said, like *Sulla* in M. de Jouy's tragedy:

'J'ai gouverné sans peur et j'abdique sans crainte' (I have ruled without fear, and I abdicate without dread), if the verse had only been better. But Albert is a man of wit, he execrates mediocre literature; which might in the end explain his anxiety to leave the Opéra-Comique.

Another great man whom I did not know, but whose reputation in Paris is immense, ruled, and I believe still rules, at the Gymnase-Dramatique. His name is Sauton. He has furthered the progress of art on a broad and new path. He has established friendly relations of equality and fraternity between the Romans and authors; a system which David too, that plagiarist, was quick to adopt. You now find the chief of the *claque* seated familiarly at the table not only of Melpomene, or Thalia, or Terpsichore, but even of Apollo and Orpheus. He pledged his signature for them, he helps them from his own purse in their secret embarrassments, he protects them, he loves them from his heart.

The following admirable speech of the emperor Sauton to one of our cleverest authors, and one of the least inclined to save up money, is quoted:

At the end of a cordial breakfast, at which the cordials had not been spared, Sauton, red with emotion, twisting up his napkin, at last found enough courage to say, without too much stuttering, to his host:—'My dear D***, I have a great favor to ask of you . . .' 'What is that? speak out!' 'Allow me to . . . thee-and-thou you . . . let us thee-and-thou each other!' 'Willingly. Sauton, lend me (prête-moi) a thousand crowns.' 'Ah! my dear friend, you(tu) enchant me!' And, pulling out his pocket-book: 'Here they are!'

I cannot draw for you, gentlemen, the portrait of all the illustrious men of the city of Rome; I have neither the time nor the biographical knowledge. I will only add to what I have said of the three heroes I have just had the honor to entertain you with, that Auguste, Albert, and Sauton, though rivals, were always united. They did not imitate, during their triumvirate, the wars and perfidy that dishonor that of Anthony, Octavius and Lepidus. Far from it; whenever there was at the Opéra one of those terrible performances at which a shining, formidable, epic victory must positively be won, a victory that Pindar and Homer would be powerless to sing, Auguste, disdaining raw recruits, would make an appeal to his triumvirs. They, proud to rush into hand to hand conflict by the side of so great a man, would consent to acknowledge him as a leader, and bring him, Albert his indomitable phalanx, Sauton his light troops, all filled with that ardor that nothing can resist, and which begets prodigies. These three select bodies were united in a single army, on the eve of the performance, in the pit of the Opéra. Auguste, with his plan, libretto in his hand, would put his troops through a laborious rehearsal, profiting at times by the remarks of Anthony and Lepidus, who had but few to make; so rapid and sure was the glance of Auguste, such penetration had he to divine the enemy's intentions, such genius to thwart them, such judgment not to attempt the impossible. And then, what a triumph on the morrow! What acclamations, what *spolia opima!* which indeed were not offered to Jupiter Stator, but came from him, on the contrary, and from twenty other gods.

Such are the priceless services rendered to art and artists by the Roman Nation.

Would you believe, gentlemen, that there has been some talk of dismissing them from the Opéra? Several newspapers announce this reform, which we shall not believe in, even if we ourselves are witnesses to it. *The claque,* in fact, has become a necessity of the times; it has introduced itself everywhere, under all forms, under all masks, under every pretext. It reigns and governs at the theatres, in the concert-room, at the clubs, in church, in industrial societies, in the press, even in the drawing-room. As soon as twenty assembled individuals are called to decide upon the deeds, actions or ideas of any one individual who attitudinizes before them, you may be sure that at least one-quarter of the Areopagus is put by the side of the remaining three-quarters to *set fire* to them, if they are inflammable, and to show its ardor alone if they are not. In the latter very frequent case, this isolated and already determined upon enthusiasm is still enough to flatter most self-loves. Some succeed in deceiving themselves about the real value of a suffrage so obtained; others do not in the least, and desire it notwithstanding. These have got to the point that, if they had no live men at command to applaud them, would yet be happy at the applause of a troupe of manikins, even at the sight of a clapping machine; they would turn the crank themselves.

The *claqueurs* at our theatres have become learned practitioners; their trade has raised itself to an art.

People have often admired, but never enough, as I think, the marvelous talent with which Auguste used to *direct* the great works of the modern *repertoire,* and the excellence of the advice he often gave their authors. Hidden in his parquet-box, he was present at every rehearsal of the artists, before having his own with his

army. Then when the *maestro* said to him: 'Here you
will give three rounds, there you will call out encore,'
he would answer with imperturbable assurance, as the
case might be: 'Sir, it is *dangerous,*' or else: 'It shall
be done,' or: 'I will think about it, my mind is not yet
made on that point. Have some *amateurs to attack with,*
and I will follow them if it *takes.*' It even happened
sometimes that Auguste would nobly resist an author
who tried to get *dangerous* applause from him, and
answer him with: 'Sir, I cannot do it. You would compromise me in the eyes of the public, in the eyes of the
artists and those of my people, who know very well
that that *ought not to be done.* I have my reputation
to guard; I, too, have some self-love. Your work is
very difficult to *direct;* I will take all possible pains,
but I do not want to *get* hissed.'

By the side of the *claqueurs,* by profession, well-
taught, sagacious, prudent, inspired, in a word artists,
we also have the occasional *claqueur,* the *claqueur* from
friendship or interest; and these will not be banished
from the Opéra. They are: simple friends, who admire
in good faith all that is to be done on the stage *before
the lamps are lighted* (it is true that this species of
friend is becoming more rare; those, on the other hand,
who disparage everything beforehand, at the time
and afterwards, multiply enormously); relations, *those
claqueurs given by nature;* editors, ferocious *claqueurs;*
and especially lovers and husbands. That is why women,
besides the host of other advantages they have over
men, have still one more chance of success than they.

For a woman can hardly applaud her husband or lover
to any purpose in a theatre or a concert-room; besides
she always has something else to do; while the husband
or lover, provided he has the least natural capacity or
some elementary notions of the art, can often, by a
clever stroke, bring about a *success of renewal* at the
theatre, that is to say, a decided success capable of forcing the director to renew an engagement. Husbands
are better than lovers for this sort of operation. The
latter usually stand in fear of ridicule; they also fear
in petto that a too brilliant success may make too many
rivals; they no longer have any pecuniary interest in
the triumphs of their mistresses; but the husband, who
holds the purse-strings, who knows what can be done
by a well-thrown bouquet, a well-carried recall, a well
taken up salvo, a well-communicated emotion, he alone
dares to account what faculties he has. He has the gift
of ventriloquism and of ubiquity. He applauds for an
instant from the amphitheatre, crying out: *Brava!* in a
tenor voice, in chest tones; thence he flies to the lobby
of the first boxes, and sticking his head through the
opening cut in the door, he throws out an *Admirable!*
in a voice *basso profundo* while passing by, and
then he bounds breathless up to the third tier, from
whence he makes the house resound with exclamations:
'Delicious! ravishing! Heavens! what talent! it is too
much!' in a *soprano* voice, in shrill feminine tones
stifled with emotion. There is a model husband for you,
and a hard-working and intelligent father of a family.
As for the husband who is a man of taste, reserved,

staying in his seat through a whole act, not daring to
applaud even the most superb efforts of his better-half,
it may be said without fear of mistake that he is a . . .
lost husband, or that his wife is an angel.

Was it not a husband who invented the *hiss of success;* the hiss of enthusiasm, the hiss at high pressure?
which is done in the following manner:

If the public, having become too familiar with the
talent of a woman who appears before them every day,
seems to fall into the apathetic indifference that is
brought on by satiety, a devoted and little-known man
is stationed in the house to wake them up. At the precise moment when the *diva* has just given manifest
proof of her talent, and when the artistic *claqueurs* are
doing their best together in the centre of the pit, a
shrill and insulting noise starts out from some obscure
corner. Then the audience rises like one man, a prey to
indignation, and the avenging plaudits burst forth with
indescribable frenzy. 'What infamy!' is shrieked on
every hand. 'What a shameful cabal! *Brava! Bravissima!*
charming! intoxicating! etc., etc.' But this daring feat
has to be skillfully performed; there are, moreover,
very few women who consent to submit to the fictitious
affront of a hiss, however productive it may be afterwards.

Such is the impression that approving or disapprov-
ing noises make upon almost all artists, even when these
noises express neither admiration nor blame. Habit,
their imagination and a little weakness of mind make
them feel joy or pain, according as the air in a theatre

is set in vibration in one or the other way. The physical phenomenon is enough, independently of any idea of glory or shame. I am certain that there are actors who are childish enough to suffer when they travel on the railway, on account of the locomotive-whistle.

The art of the *claque* even reacts upon musical composition. It is the numerous varieties of Italian *claqueurs,* either amateurs or artists, that have brought composers to finish all their pieces by that redundant, trivial, ridiculous period that is called *cabaletta,* little cabal, which provokes applause, and is always the same. When the *cabaletta* was no longer enough for them, they introduced the big-drum, the big cabal, which at the present day destroys both music and singers. When they got blasé with the big-drum and found themselves powerless to *carry* the success by the old means, they at last demanded of the poor *maestri* duets, trios and choruses in unison. In some passages they even had to put both voices and orchestra in unison, thus producing an *ensemble* piece in *one* single part, but in which the enormous sonority seems preferable to all harmony, to all instrumentation, to every musical idea, in a word, for *carrying away* the public, and making it believe itself electrified.

Analogous examples abound in the manufacture of literary works.

As for the dancers, their business is perfectly simple; it is agreed upon with the *impresario:* 'You will give me so many thousand francs per month, so many *passes* per performance, and the *claque* will give me a *recep-*

tion and *exit,* and two rounds at each of my *echos.'*

By means of the *claque,* directors make or unmake
at will what is still called a success. A single word to
the chief of the parterre is enough to undo an artist
who has not a talent out of the common run. I remember Auguste saying one evening at the Opéra, passing
through the ranks of his army before the curtain rose:
'Nothing for M. Dérivis! nothing for M. Dérivis!'
The order went round, and during the whole evening
Dérivis did not get a single bit of applause. When the
director wishes to get rid of a member of his company
for some reason or other, he employs this ingenious
method, and, after two or three performances at which
there *has been nothing* for M**** or Madame***:
'You see,' says he to the artist, 'I cannot keep you; your
talent is not sympathetic to the public.' It happens, on
the other hand, that these tactics miscarry sometimes
in the case of an artist of the first rank. 'Nothing for
him!' has been said at the official centre. But the
public, astonished at first at the silence of the Romans, soon begins to see where the shoe pinches, and
sets itself to work most officiously, and with all the
more warmth, now that it has a hostile cabal to thwart.
The artist then has an exceptional success, a *circular*
success, the centre of the pit having no hand in it. But
I should not dare to say whether he is more proud of
this spontaneous enthusiasm of the public, or angry at
the inaction of the *claque.*

To dream of suddenly destroying such an institution
in the largest of our theatres, seems to me to be as im-

possible and insane, as to try to annihilate a religion between this evening and to-morrow.

Can people imagine the disarray of the Opéra? the discouragement, the melancholy, the atrophy, the spleen into which the whole dancing, singing, walking, running, painting and composing people would fall? the disgust of life that would seize hold upon the gods and demi-gods, if a frightful silence should follow every *cabaletta* that was not irreproachably sung or danced? Do people think of the rage of all mediocrity at the sight of true talent getting some applause, while it, that always used to be applauded, cannot now get a hand? It would be as much as recognizing the principle of inequality, and giving a palpable proof of it; and we are a Republic; the word *Equality* is written upon the pediment of the Opéra! Besides, who would recall the leading artist after the third and fifth acts? Who would laugh when some character actor said something silly? Who would cry out: All! All! at the end of a performance? Who would cover up the bad note of a bass or tenor with obliging applause, and thus prevent the public from hearing it? It is fit to make a man shudder. Besides, the manoeuvres of the *claque* add interest to the spectacle; people enjoy seeing them at work. This is so true that, if the *claqueurs* were expelled at certain performances, not a person would remain in the house.

No, the suppression of the Romans in France is fortunately a mad dream. The heavens and the earth shall pass away, but Rome is immortal, and the *claque* shall not pass away.

On the Claque

Just listen! . . . *our prima-donna* has taken it into her head to sing with soul, simplicity and good taste the only distinguished melody that is to be found in this poor opera. You will see, she will not get any applause. . . . Ah! I was wrong; yes, they are applauding her; but how? How badly it is done! What an abortion of a salvo, badly attacked, and badly taken up! There is good will enough in the audience, but no science, no *ensemble,* and consequently no effect. If Auguste had had that woman to *care for,* he would have carried the whole house in a trice, and you yourselves, who have no notion of applauding, would have been drawn into his enthusiasm willy-nilly.

I have not yet drawn for you the portrait of a Roman woman; I will do that during the last act of our opera, which will begin soon. Let us have a short *entr'acte;* I am tired.

(The musicians go off a few steps, talking over their reflections in a low voice, while the curtain falls. But three raps of the conductor's *baton* upon his desk announcing the continuation of the performance, my audience groups itself attentively about me.)

Madame Rosenhain
Another Fragment of Roman History

An opera in five acts was *ordered* some years ago of a French composer, whom you do not know, by M. Duponchel. While the last rehearsals were going on, I was reflecting, at my fireside, upon the anguish the un-

263

fortunate composer of this opera was then *occupied* in experiencing. I thought of the ever-renewed torments of every description that no one escapes in Paris in such cases, neither the great nor the small, the patient nor the irritable, the humble nor the proud, neither German, Frenchman, nor even Italian. I pictured to myself the atrociously slow rehearsals at which the sad composer thinks himself bound to laugh heartily while death is in his soul, ridiculous sallies which he bestirs himself to answer with the heaviest and dullest stupidities he can think of, that those of the singers may have more point and so seem something akin to wit. I heard the director's voice reprimanding him, treating him like a child, reminding him of the extreme honor they did his work in troubling themselves about it so long; threatening him with its utter and complete abandonment if all were not ready on the fixed day; I saw the slave paralyzed with fear, and blushing at the eccentric reflections of his master (the director) upon music and musicians, at his nonsensical theories of melody, rhythm, instrumentation and style; theories in the exposition of which the director, as usual, treated the great masters like idiots, and idiots like great masters, and mistook the Piraeus for a man. Then the mezzo-soprano's leave of absence, and the illness of the bass were announced; they proposed a new beginner to take the part of the artist, and to have a chorus-singer rehearse the leading role. And the composer felt himself choking, but took care not to complain. Oh! the hail, the rain, the icy wind, the woods stripped of their foliage by the winter's breeze, the dark squalls, the muddy sloughs, the ditches covered over by a treacherous crust, the gnawings of hunger, the frights of solitude and night, how sweet it is to think of them in some lodging-place, were it even as poor as that of the hare in the fable, in the repose of luke-warm inaction; to feel one's sense of comfort *redouble at the far-off noise of the tempest,* and to repeat, while stroking one's beard and luxuriously closing one's eyes like a priest's cat, that prayer of the German poet Henri Heine, a prayer, alas! that is so seldom heard: 'O Lord! thou knowest that I have an excellent heart, that I am full of pity and sympathy for the woes of others; grant then, if it please thee, that my neighbor may have my ills to endure; I will surround him with such care, such delicate attentions; my pity will be so active, so ingenious, that he will bless thy right hand, Lord, while receiving such sweet consolation. But to load me with the weight of my own sufferings! to make me suffer myself! Oh! it would be frightful! take away from my lips, great God, this cup of bitterness!'

I was thus plunged in pious meditations, when somebody rapped lightly at the door of my oratory. My *valet-de-chambre* being on a mission to a foreign court, I asked myself if I were at home, and, on my reply in the affirmative, I opened the door. A lady appeared, very well dressed and, faith, not too young; she was in all the bloom of her forty-fifth year. I saw at once that she was an artist; there are infallible signs by which these unhappy victims of inspiration are to be known.

'Sir, you have lately conducted a grand concert at Versailles, and, up to the last day, I hoped to take part in it . . . ; but what is done is done.' 'Madame, the program was drawn by the committee of the Association of Musicians; I am not to blame for it. Besides, Madame Dorus-Gras and Madame Widemann . . .' 'Oh! those ladies, no doubt, said nothing; but it is no less true that they were probably very much displeased.' 'With what, if you please?' 'That I was not engaged.' 'You think so?' 'I am sure of it. But let us not recriminate on that head. I came, sir, to beg you to be kind enough to recommend me to MM. Roqueplan and Duponchel; my intention is to get an engagement at the Opéra. I was attached to the Théâtre-Italien until last season, and certainly, I can only be proud of the excellent behavior of M. Vatel; but since the revolution of February . . . , you understand that such a theatre cannot do for me.' 'Madame has, no doubt, good reasons for being severe in her choice of co-workers; but if I might express an opinion . . .' 'Useless, sir, my mind is made up, irrevocably made up; it is impossible for me to remain at the Théâtre-Italien under any conditions whatever. Every thing there is profoundly antipathetic to me—the public that comes there, and the public that does not come there; and, although the present condition of the Opéra is hardly brilliant, as my son and both my daughters were engaged there last year by the new direction, I should be very glad to be admitted there, and shall not haggle about the appointments.' 'You forget, I see, that as the directors of the Opéra have an excessively superficial knowledge, and a very vague sentiment for music, they naturally have fixed ideas concerning our art, and consequently attach very little value to recommendations, to mine especially. But still, be so good as to tell me what your voice is.' 'I do not sing.' 'Then I shall have still less credit since it concerns the ballet.' 'I do not dance.' 'Then it is only among walking ladies that you wish admittance?' 'I do not walk, sir; You strangely misunderstand me' (*smiling with a touch of irony*). 'I am Madame Rosenhain.' 'Any relation to the pianist?' 'No, but Mesdames Persiane, Grisi, Alboni, MM. Mario and Tamburini must have spoken to you about me, seeing that I have, for six years, played a prominent part in their triumphs. I had thought for an instant of going to London to give lessons, as they tell me that they are very moderately advanced over there; but I repeat as my children are at the Opéra . . . , and then the size of the theatre thrown open to my ambition . . .' 'Excuse my want of sagacity madam, and be so good as to tell me at last what your special talent is!' 'Sir, I am an artist who has made M. Vatel make more money than Rubini himself, and I flatter myself that I can bring about the most favorable reaction in the receipts of the opera, if my two daughters, who have already attracted attention, profit by my example. I am, sir, a *flower-thrower.*' 'Ah! very well! you are in the Enthusiasm?' 'Precisely. This branch of musical art has hardly begun to flourish. Formerly it was the ladies of the upper circles who practiced it, and that nearly gratuitously. You may re-

member the concerts of M. Liszt and the first appearances of M. Duprez. What volleys of bouquets! What
applause! You saw young girls, and even married
women, become enthusiastic without regard for modesty; several among them gravely compromised themselves more than once. But what a tumult! what disorder! what quantities of beautiful flowers lost! it was
a fearful pity! To-day, as the public no longer put their
finger into the pie at all, thanks to heaven and the
artists, we have regulated all ovations according to my
system, and it is quite another thing.

'Under the last direction of the Opéra our art came
near being lost, or at the very least, going backward.
They intrusted the part of Enthusiasm to four young,
inexperienced dancers, who were personally known to
all the *habitués* into the bargain; these children, new
to the business, as girls are at that age, took their sta-
tions in the house always in the same places, and always
threw the same bouquets at the same moment to the
same cantatrice; so that at last people began to turn
the eloquence of their flowers to derision. My daughters, profiting by my lessons, have reformed that, and
I think that now the administration has reason to be
entirely satisfied.'

'Is your son also in the flower business?' 'Oh, as for
my son, he excites enthusiasm in another way: he has a
superb voice.'

'Then why is his name not known to me?'

'He is never down on the posters.'

'But he sings?'

'No, sir, he screams, and in difficult cases his voice has often sufficed to carry away the most recalcitrant masses; my son, sir, is for the *recalls.*'

'What can he be, a countryman of O'Connell? I do not know that actor.'

'My son is for the recall of the leading artists when the audience remains cold and does not recall anybody. You see that he has no sinecure, and that he earns his money well. He had the good fortune, when he made his first appearances at the Théâtre-Français, to find a tragedian there whose name begins with an excellent syllable, the syllable Ra! God knows all the account this Ra! can be turned to! I should have been very anxious about his success at the Opéra when I heard of the retirement of the famous cantatrice whose single *O* resounded so well, in spite of the five Teutonic consonants that surround it, if there had not come another *prima-donna,* whose still more advantageous syllable, the syllable Ma, placed my son upon the very pinnacle of success at the first dash. Now you know all.'

'Completely. I will tell you, madam, that your talent is the best of all recommendations; that the direction of the Opéra will know how to appreciate it, but that you must present yourself as soon as possible, for they are on the lookout for artists like yourself, and for eight days they have been engaged in the composition of a grand enthusiasm for a third act, in which they take a lively interest.'

'Thank you, sir, thank you; I fly to the Opéra.'

And the young artist vanished. I have not heard of her since, but I got a proof of the entire success of her application, and the certainty of her making an excellent engagement with the direction of the Opéra. At the first performance of the new work which M. Duponchel had ordered, a perfect avalanche of flowers fell after the third act, and it was easily to be seen by all that they fell from a practiced hand. Unfortunately this gracious ovation did not prevent both piece and music from doing as much.' ('From doing . . . what?' said Bacon, the simple asker of questions. 'From falling flat, you idiot,' answered Corsino, roughly. 'Come now! your wit is enormously more obtuse than usual this evening! Go to bed, Basilio.')

I have now, gentlemen, to explain to you the technical terms most frequently used in the Roman language, terms which only Parisians understand:

TO GET INTO AN OVEN (*faire four*) means to produce no effect, to fall flat on the indifference of the audience.

TO HEAT AN OVEN (*chauffer un four*) is to applaud to no purpose an artist whose talent is powerless to move an audience; this expression is the pendant to that of: *Beating the air.*

TO BE COMFORTABLE (*avoir de l'agrément*) is to be applauded both by the *claque* and by part of the public. Duprez was extraordinarily *comfortable* the day of his first appearance in *Guillaume Tell.*

270

On the Claque

TO CHEER UP (*égayer*) anybody is to hiss him. This irony is cruel, but it has a hidden meaning that gives it still more edge. No doubt the unlucky artist who gets hissed only experiences a very questionable cheerfulness from the fact, but his rival in the business is cheered up by hearing him hissed, and many other people laugh, *in petto,* at the accident. So that, taken all in all, when any one is hissed, there is always some one cheered up, too.

A PULL (*tirage*) means, in the Roman language, difficulty, work, trouble. Thus the Roman says: 'It is a fine work, but we shall have a *pull* to make it go.' Which means that, in spite of all its merit, the work is tiresome, and that it will be only by great efforts that the *claque* can give it the semblance of success.

TO MAKE A RECEPTION (*faire une entrée*) is to applaud an actor as soon as he comes upon the stage, before he has opened his mouth.

TO MAKE AN EXIT (*faire une sortie*) is to pursue him with plaudits and bravos when he leaves the stage, no matter what his last gesture, his last word or scream may have been.

TO SHELTER (*mettre à couvert*) a singer is to applaud him with violent acclamations at the exact moment when he is about to give out a false or cracked note, that the bad note may be thus covered by the noise of the *claque* and that the public may not hear it.

TO SHOW CONSIDERATION (*avoir des égards*) for

271

an artist is to applaud him moderately, even when he has not been able to give any money to the *claque*. It means to encourage him *from friendship,* or *for love.* These last two expressions are equivalent to *gratis.*

TO MAKE FOAM UP WELL, or FROM THE BOTTOM (*faire mousser solidement,* or, *à fond*) is to applaud with frenzy, with hands, feet, voice and speech. During the *entr'actes,* in such cases, the work or artist must be extolled in the lobbies, in the refreshment rooms, at the neighboring café, at the cigar-shop, everywhere. One must say: 'It is a masterpiece; he has an unique talent, perfectly bewildering! an unrivaled voice! nothing like it has ever been heard!' There is a well-known professor whom the directors of the Paris Opéra always have come from abroad on solemn occasions, to make great works *foam up from the bottom,* by *kindling* the lobbies in a masterly manner. The talent of this Roman master is serious; his seriousness is admirable.

Both these last operations combined are expressed by the words CARE, to CARE FOR (*soins, soigner*).

TO GET . . . LAID HOLD OF (*faire empoigner*) is to applaud a weak thing or artist at the wrong time, which provokes the anger of the public. It sometimes happens that a mediocre cantatrice, but one who has power over the director's heart, sings most deplorably. Seated in the centre of the pit, with a sad, overpowered air, the emperor bows his head, thus indicating to his praetorians that they must keep silence, give no sign of satisfaction, unite, in a word, in his sorrowful reflec-

On the Claque

tions! But the *diva* does not at all appreciate this prudent reserve; she leaves the stage in a fury, and runs
to complain to the director of the stupidity or treason
of the *claque*. The director then gives the order that
the Roman army shall work vigorously in the next act.
To his great regret Caesar sees himself forced to obey.
The second act begins, the angry goddess sings more
false than before; three hundred pairs of devoted hands
applaud her all the same; the public, in a fury, answer
these manifestations by a symphony of hisses and Kent-
ish fire, instrumented in the modern style, and of the
most ear-splitting sonority.

I think that the use of this expression only goes back
to the reign of Charles X, and the memorable *séance*
of the Chamber of Deputies, at which a parliamentary
thunder-storm broke out, when Manuel allowed himself to say that France had seen the return of the Bour-
bons with *repugnance,* and M. de Foucault called his
gendarmes and said to them, pointing out Manuel:
'Lay hold of that man there!'

They also say, to denote this disastrous calling forth
of hisses, GET AZOR CALLED (*faire appeler Azor*);
from the custom of old ladies whistling when they call
their dog, who always bears the name of *Azor*.

I have seen Auguste, in despair after one of these
catastrophes, ready to kill himself, like Brutus at
Philippi. . . . One consideration alone restrained him:
he was necessary to his art and country; he must live
for them.

273

Berlioz*Berlioz*

TO CONDUCT (*conduire*) a work, is to direct the operations of the Roman army during the performances of such work.

BRRRRRR! This noise, which the emperor makes with his mouth in directing certain movements of his troops, and which all his lieutenants can hear, is a signal for them to give extraordinary rapidity to their clapping, and to accompany it with stamping. It is the command to make *foam up well*.

The motion from right to left and from left to right of the imperial head, illumined with a smile, is the signal for moderate laughter.

Caesar's two hands clapped together vigorously and raised for a moment in the air, command a sudden burst of laughter.

If the hands stay in the air longer than usual, the laugh must be prolonged and followed by a round of applause.

HM! thrown out in a certain way, provokes emotion in Caesar's soldiers; they must at such times put on a mollified look, and let fall, with some tears, a murmur of approbation.

There, gentlemen, is all that I can tell you about the illustrious men and women of the city of Rome. I have not lived long enough among them to know more. Excuse the short-comings of the historian.

The amateur in the stalls thanks me most overwhelmingly; he has not lost a word of my story, and I

274

have noticed him furtively taking notes. The gas is put out, and we go away. In coming down stairs: 'You do not know who the inquisitive old boy is who asked you about the Romans?' said Dimsky, the first double-bass, with an air of mystery. 'No.' 'He is the director of the theatre in *****; you may be sure that he will profit by all he has heard this evening, and will found an institution in his own town similar to that in Paris.' 'All right! in that case I am sorry that I did not call his attention to rather an important fact. The directors of the Opéra, those of the Opéra-Comique and of the Théâtre-Français, have gone into partnership to found a Conservatoire, so as to have an experienced young man, a real Caesar, or, at the very least, a young Octavius, at the head of the institution.'

'I will write him that; I know him.

'You had better, my dear Dimsky.

'Let us all *care* for our art, and watch over the safety of the empire. Good night!'

SEP 1 0 1982